This Book Belongs To

____

____

Practice Writing Your Own Story

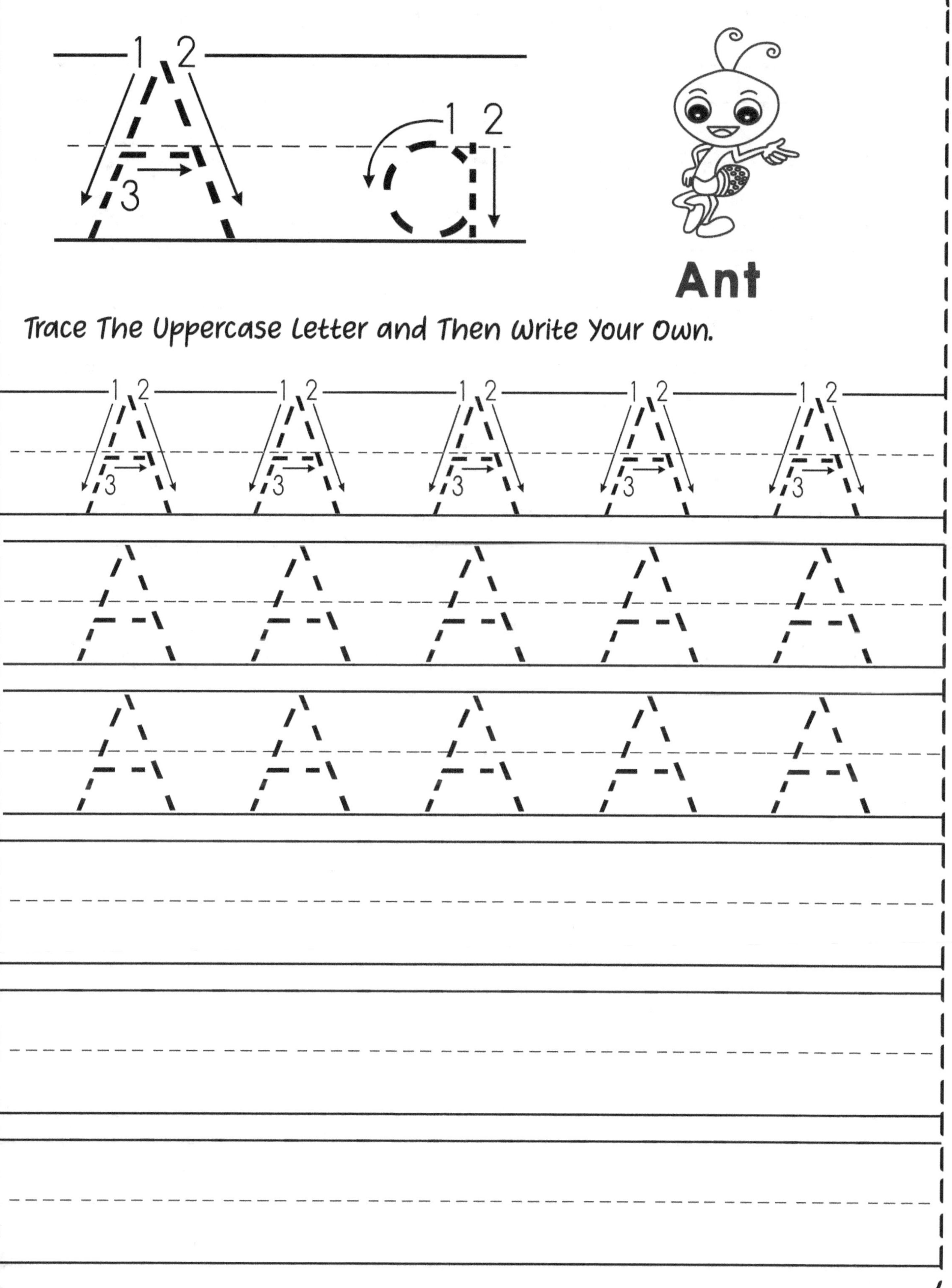

Trace The Uppercase Letter and Then Write Your Own.

Ant

Trace The Lowercase Letter and Then Write Your Own.

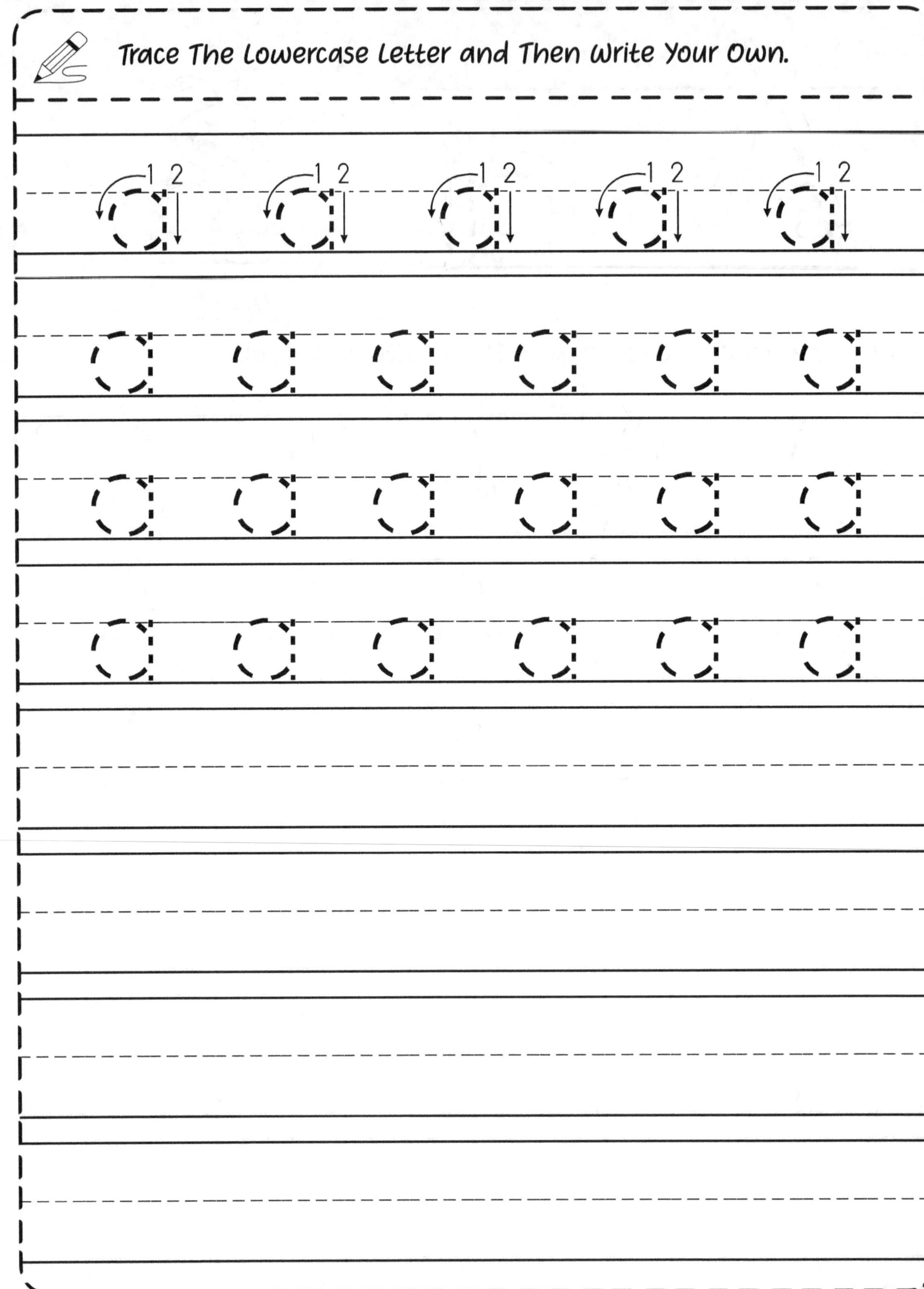

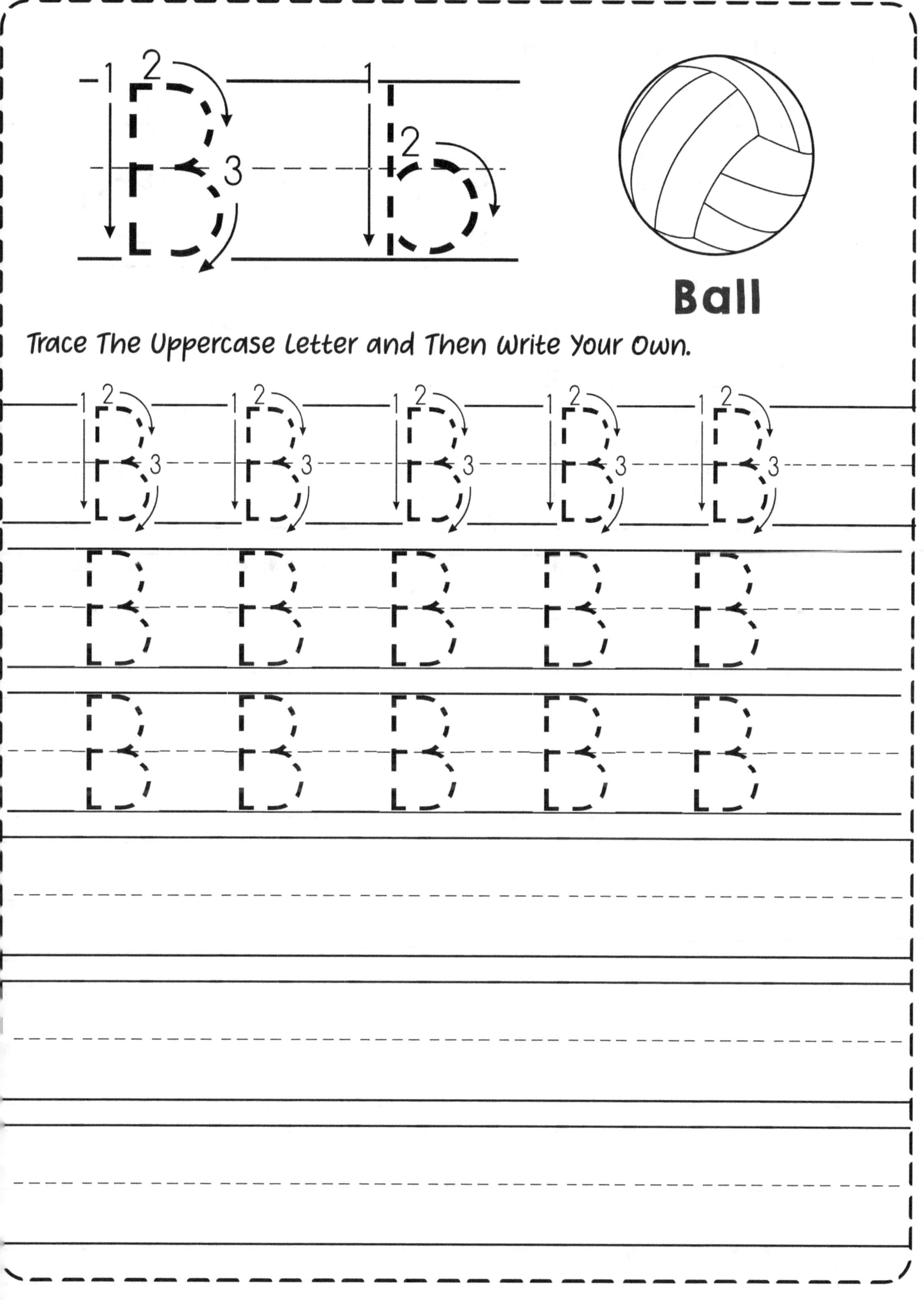

Trace The Uppercase Letter and Then Write Your Own.

Trace The Lowercase Letter and Then Write Your Own.

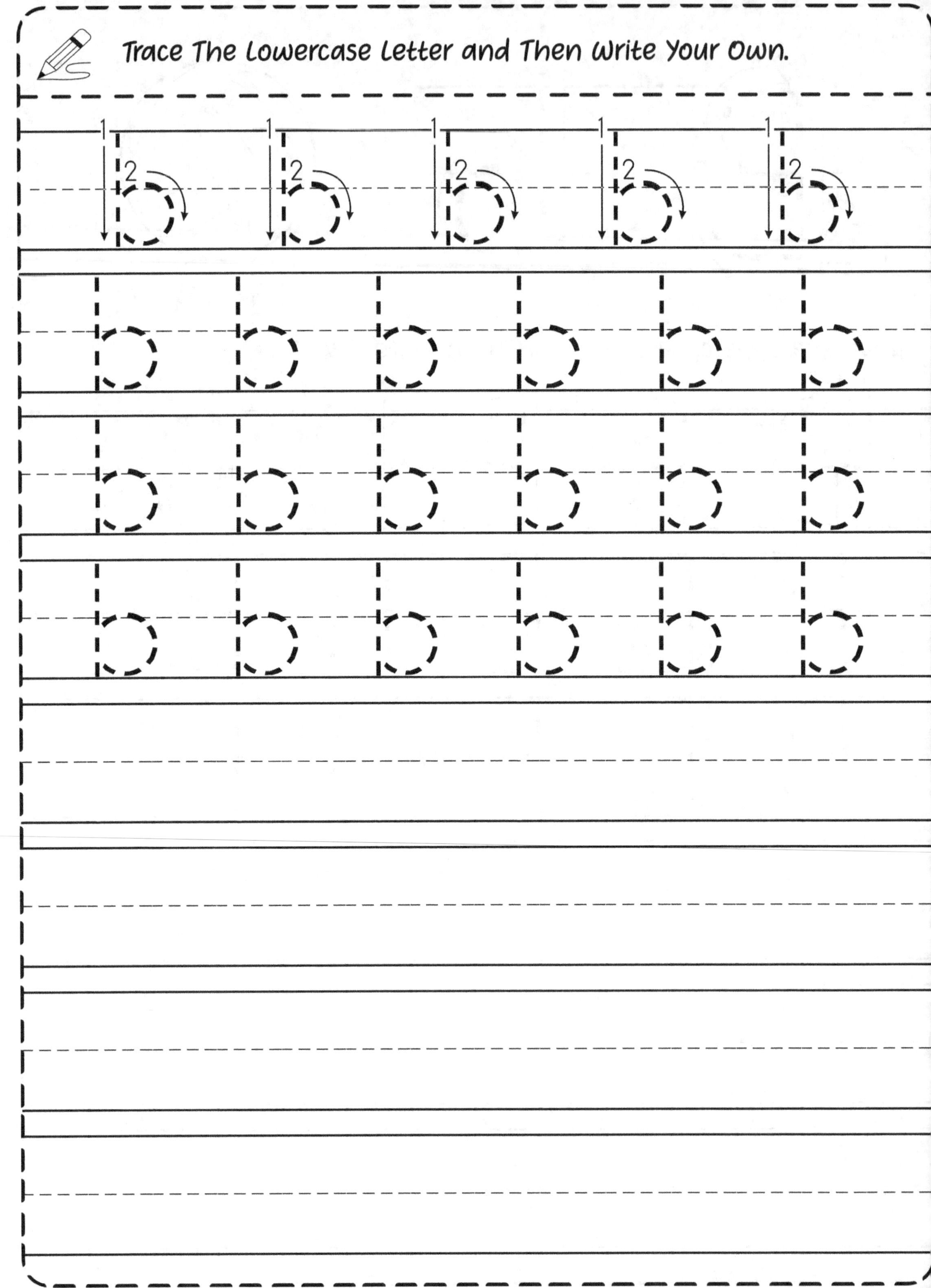

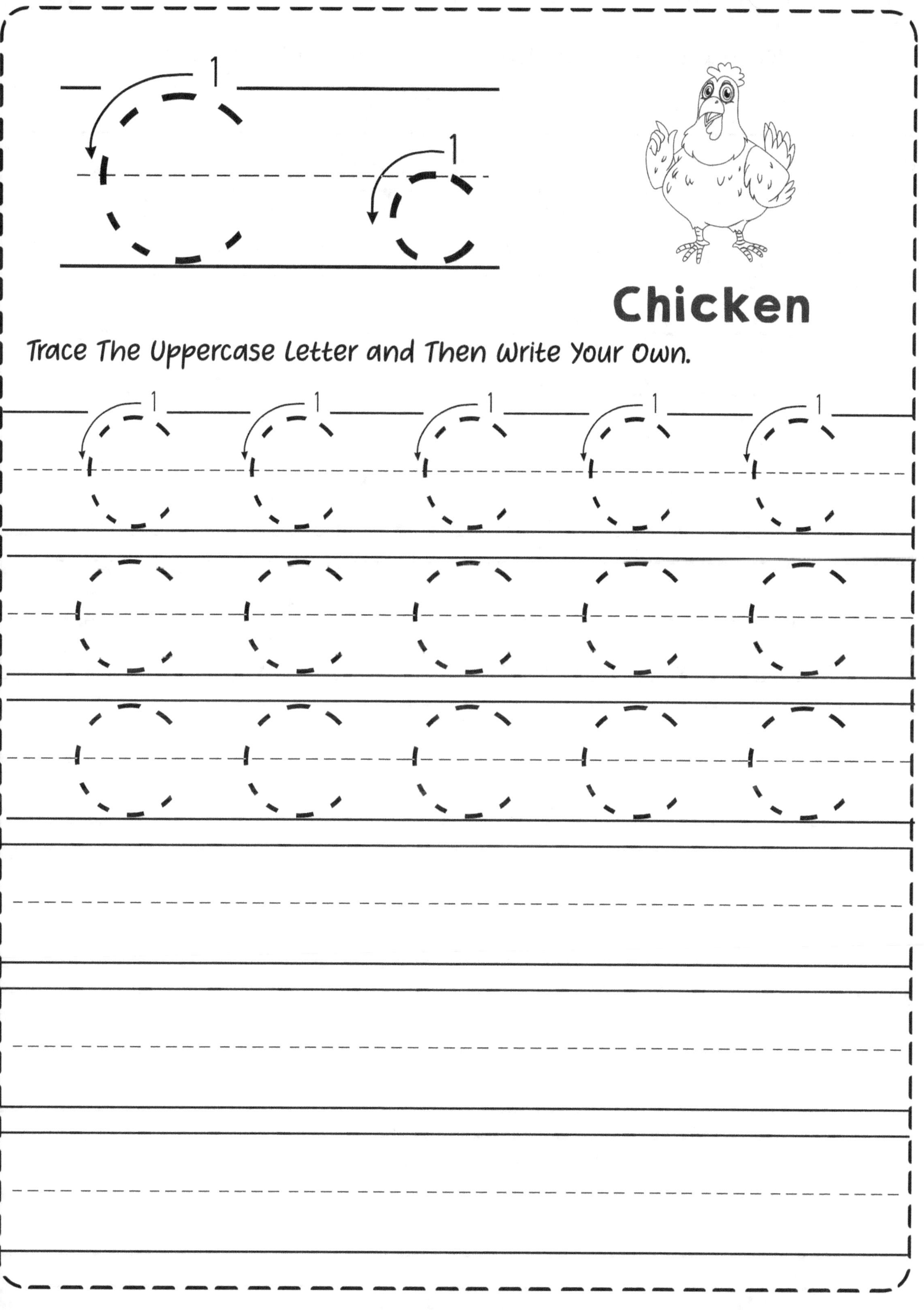

Chicken

Trace The Uppercase Letter and Then Write Your Own.

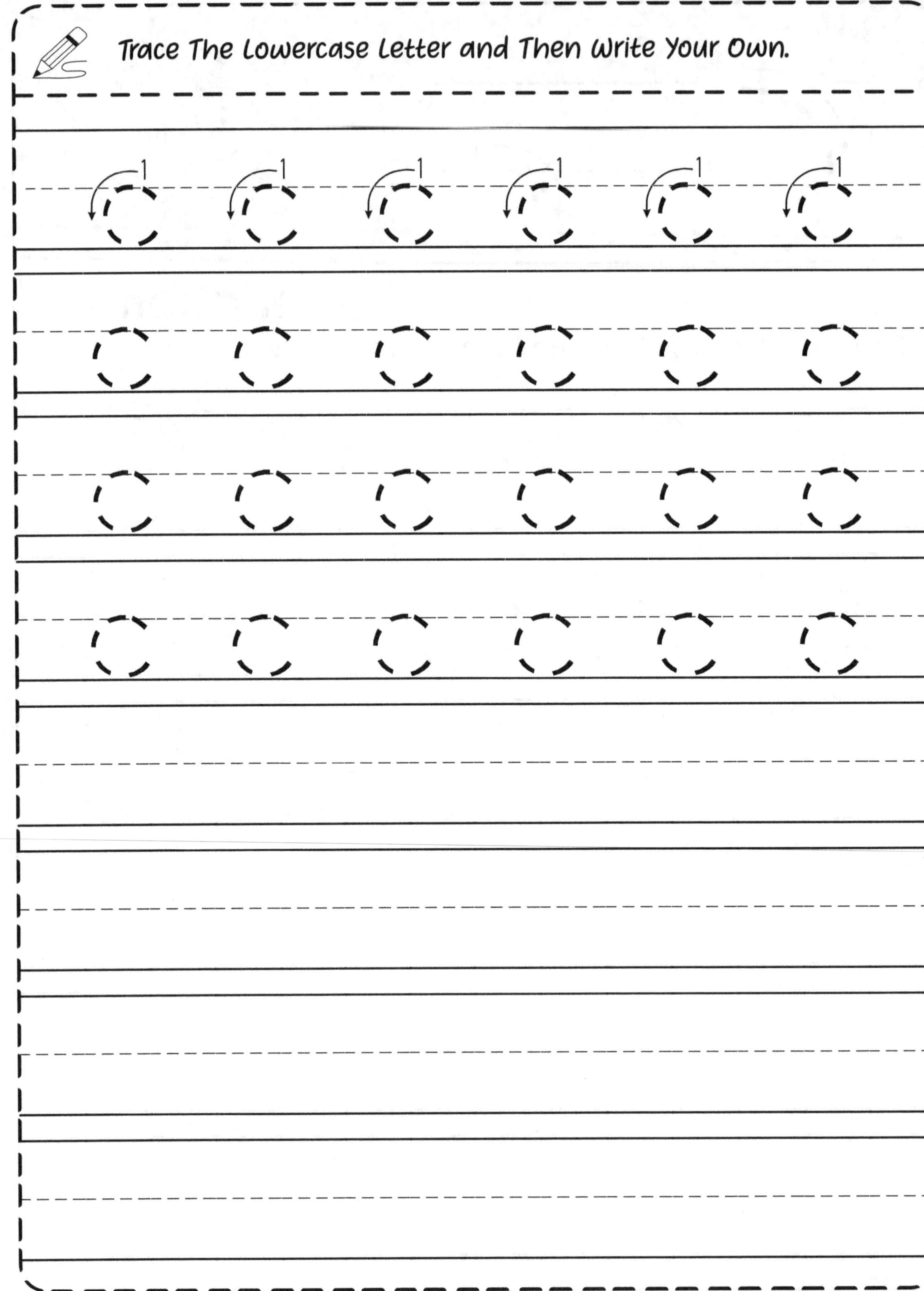

Trace The Lowercase Letter and Then Write Your Own.

Duck
Trace The Uppercase Letter and Then Write Your Own.

Trace The Lowercase Letter and Then Write Your Own.

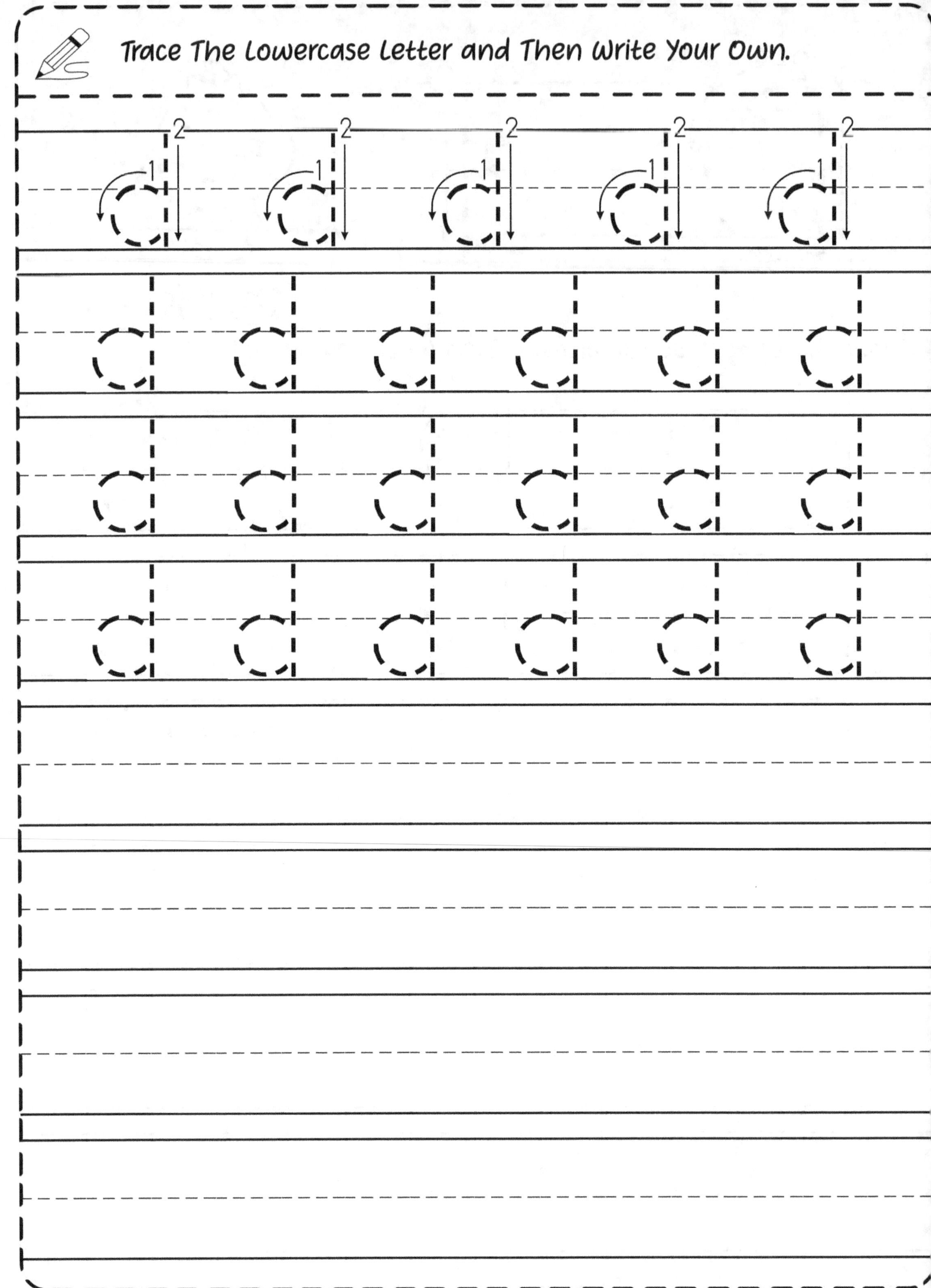

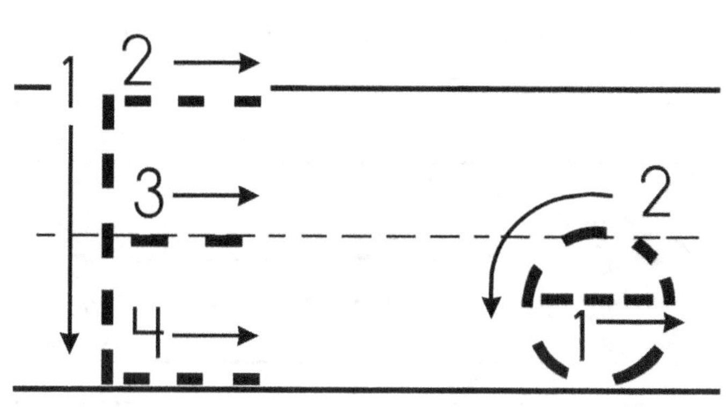

Eggplant

Trace The Uppercase Letter and Then Write Your Own.

Trace The Lowercase Letter and Then Write Your Own.

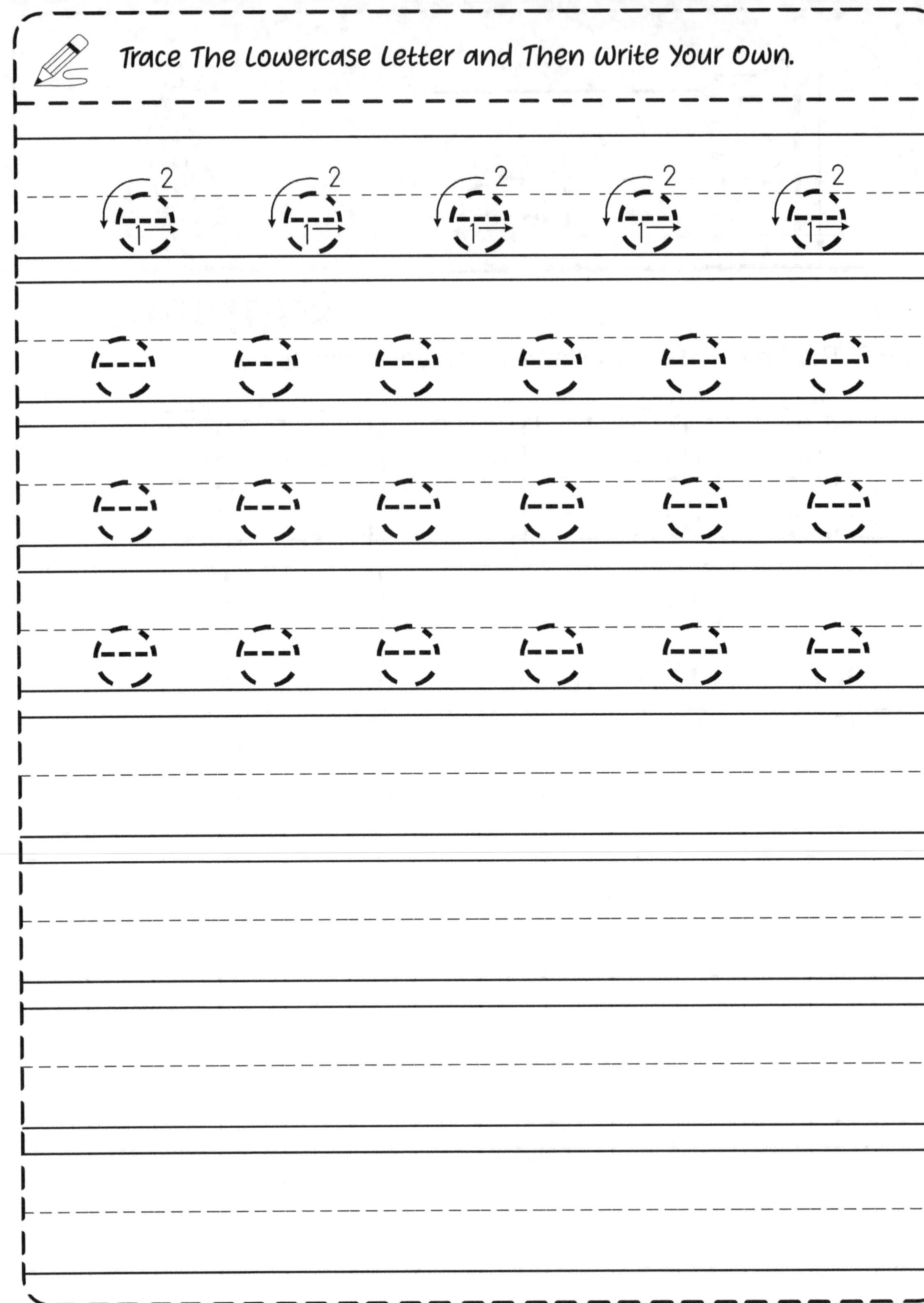

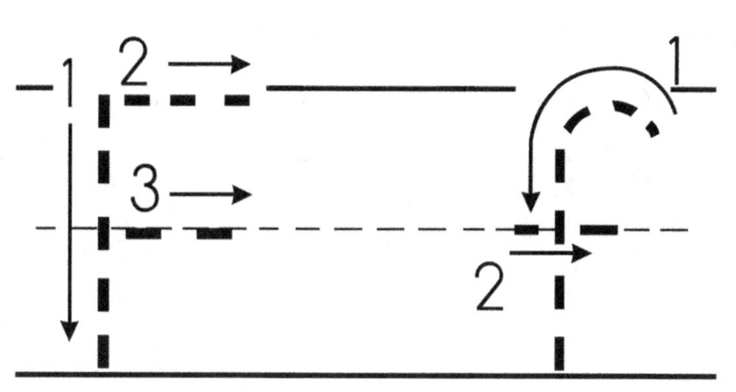

Flower

Trace The Uppercase Letter and Then Write Your Own.

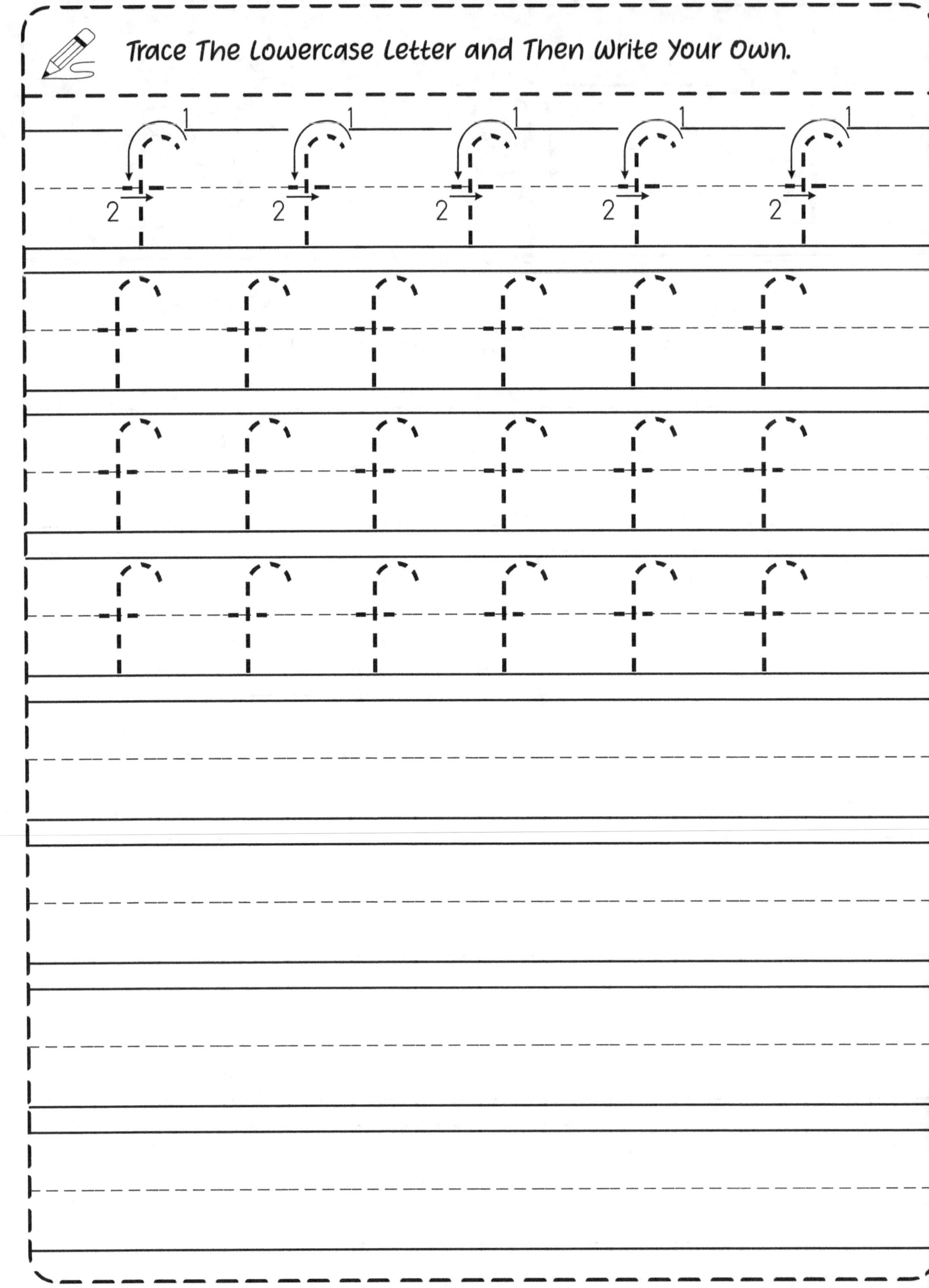

Trace The Lowercase Letter and Then Write Your Own.
1
2
1
2
1
2
1
2
1
2

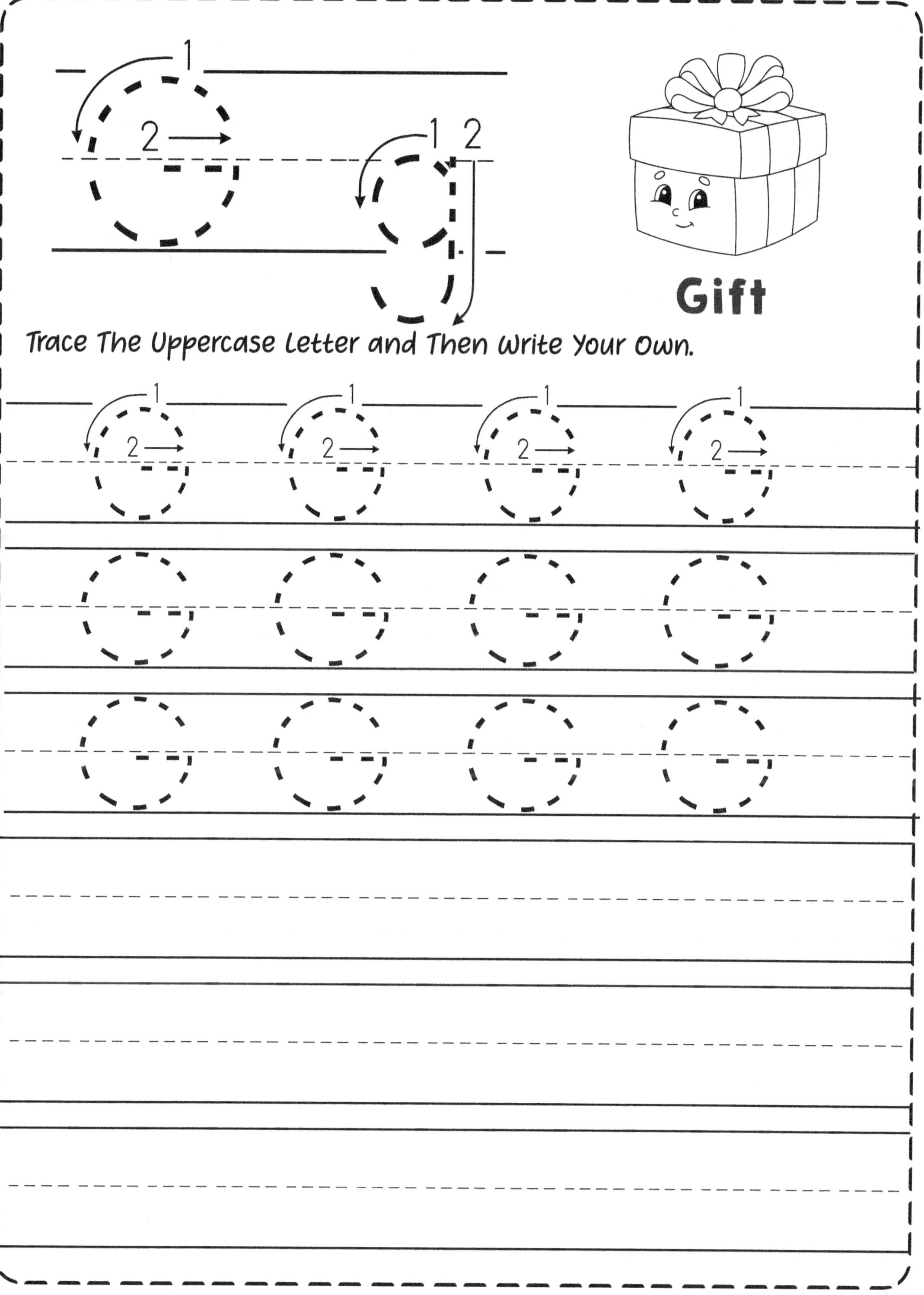

Gift

Trace The Uppercase Letter and Then Write Your Own.

Trace The Lowercase Letter and Then Write Your Own.

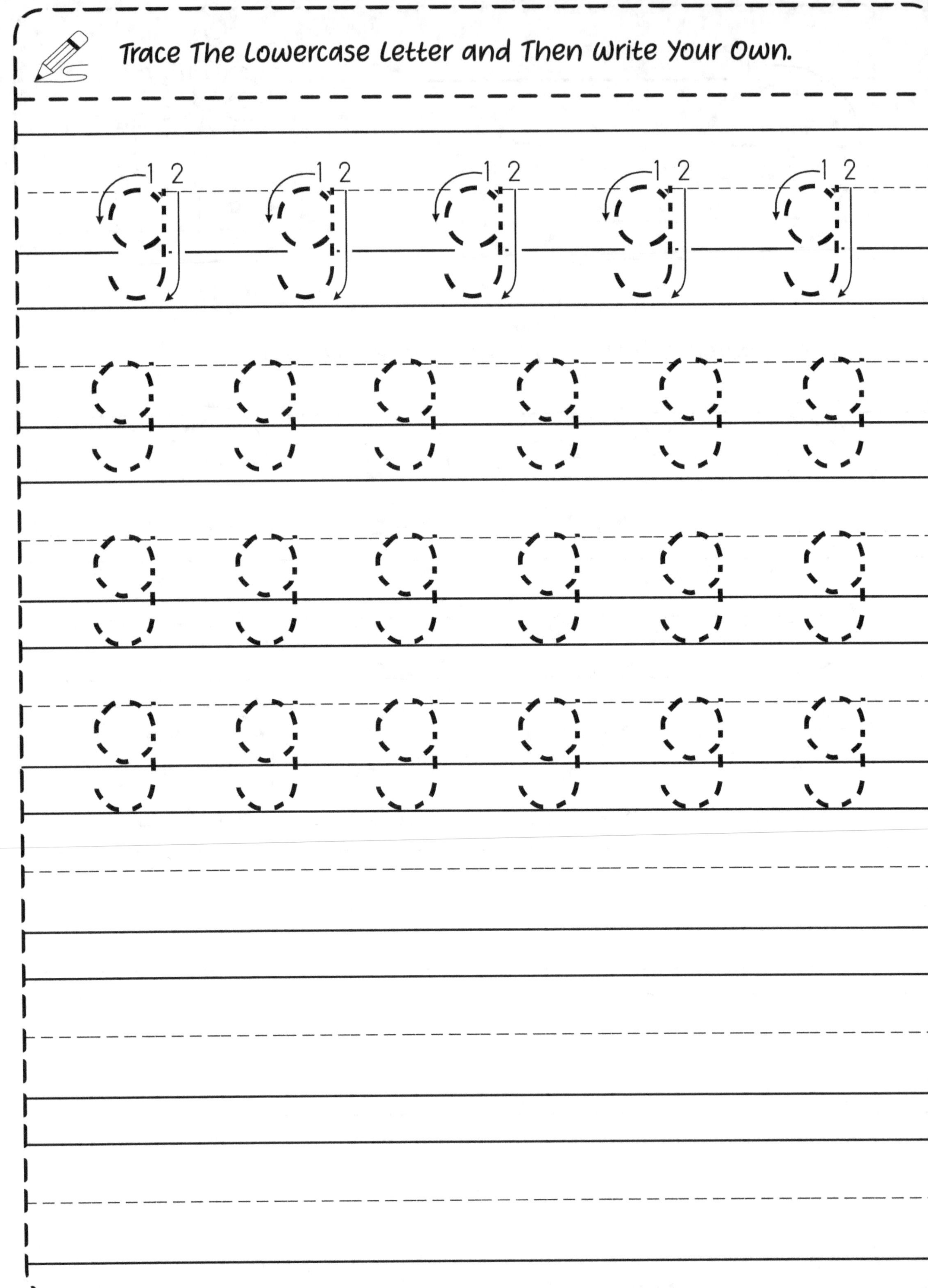

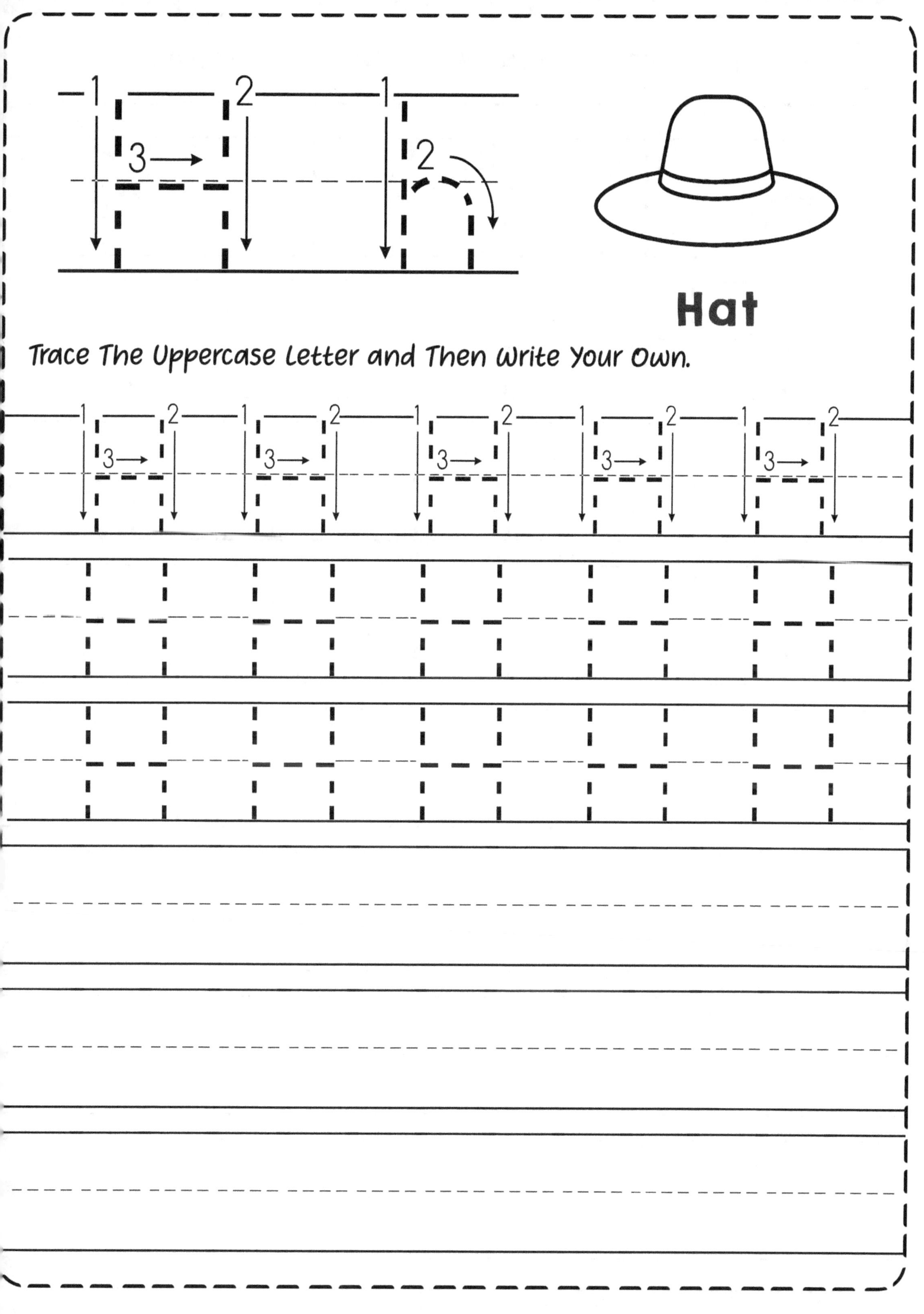

Hat

Trace The Uppercase Letter and Then Write Your Own.

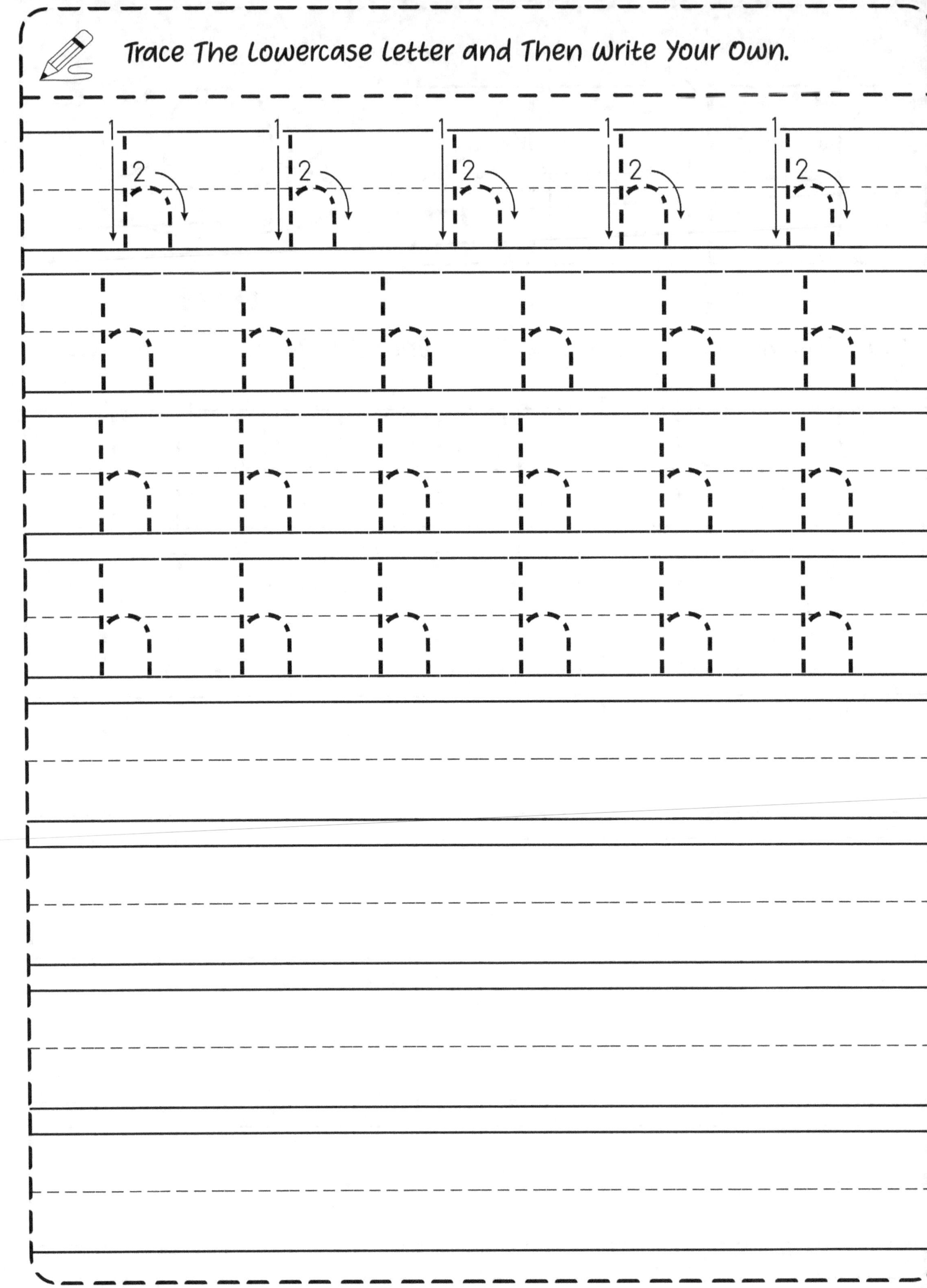

Trace The Lowercase Letter and Then Write Your Own.

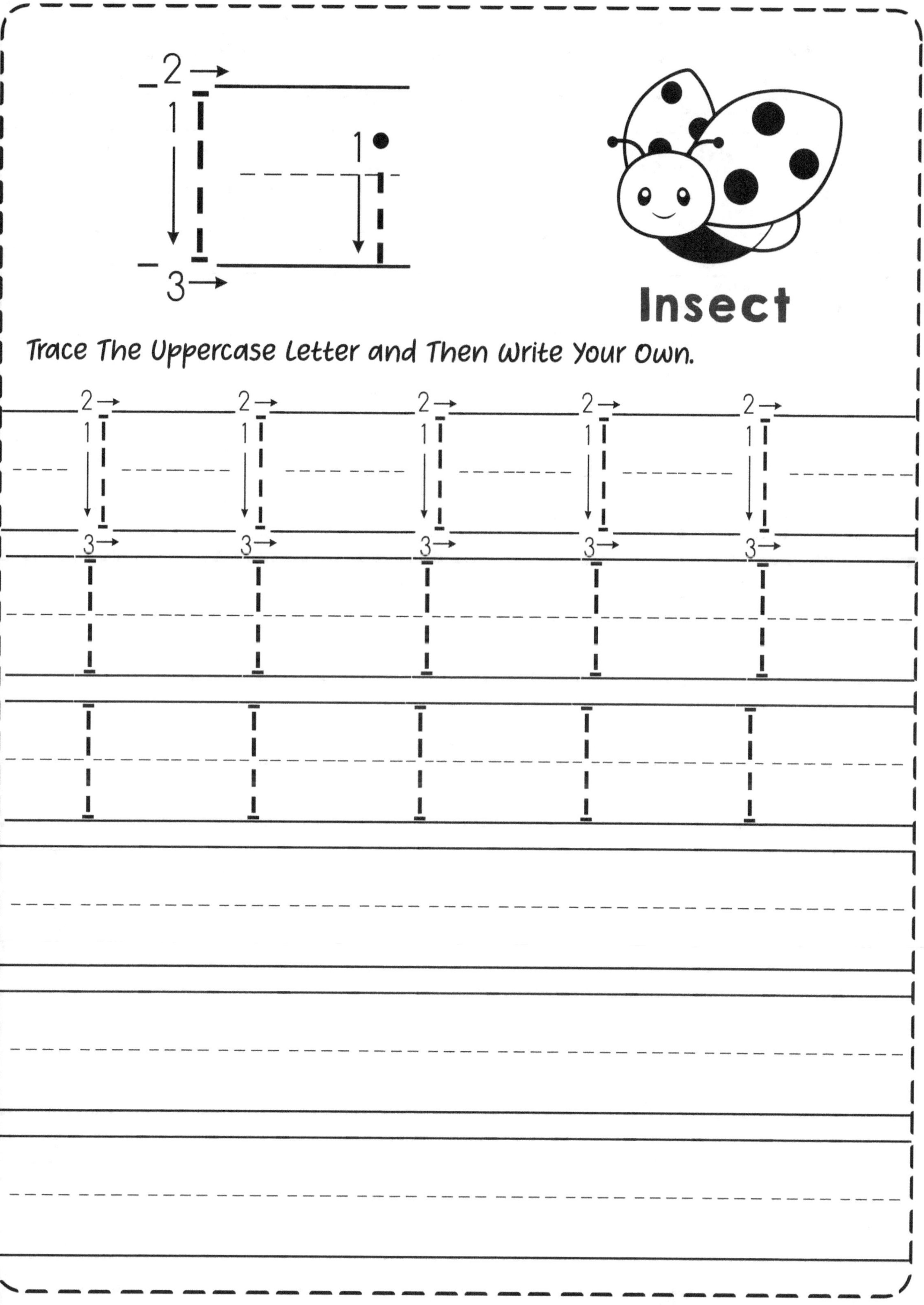

Insect

Trace The Uppercase Letter and Then Write Your Own.

Trace The Lowercase Letter and Then Write Your Own.

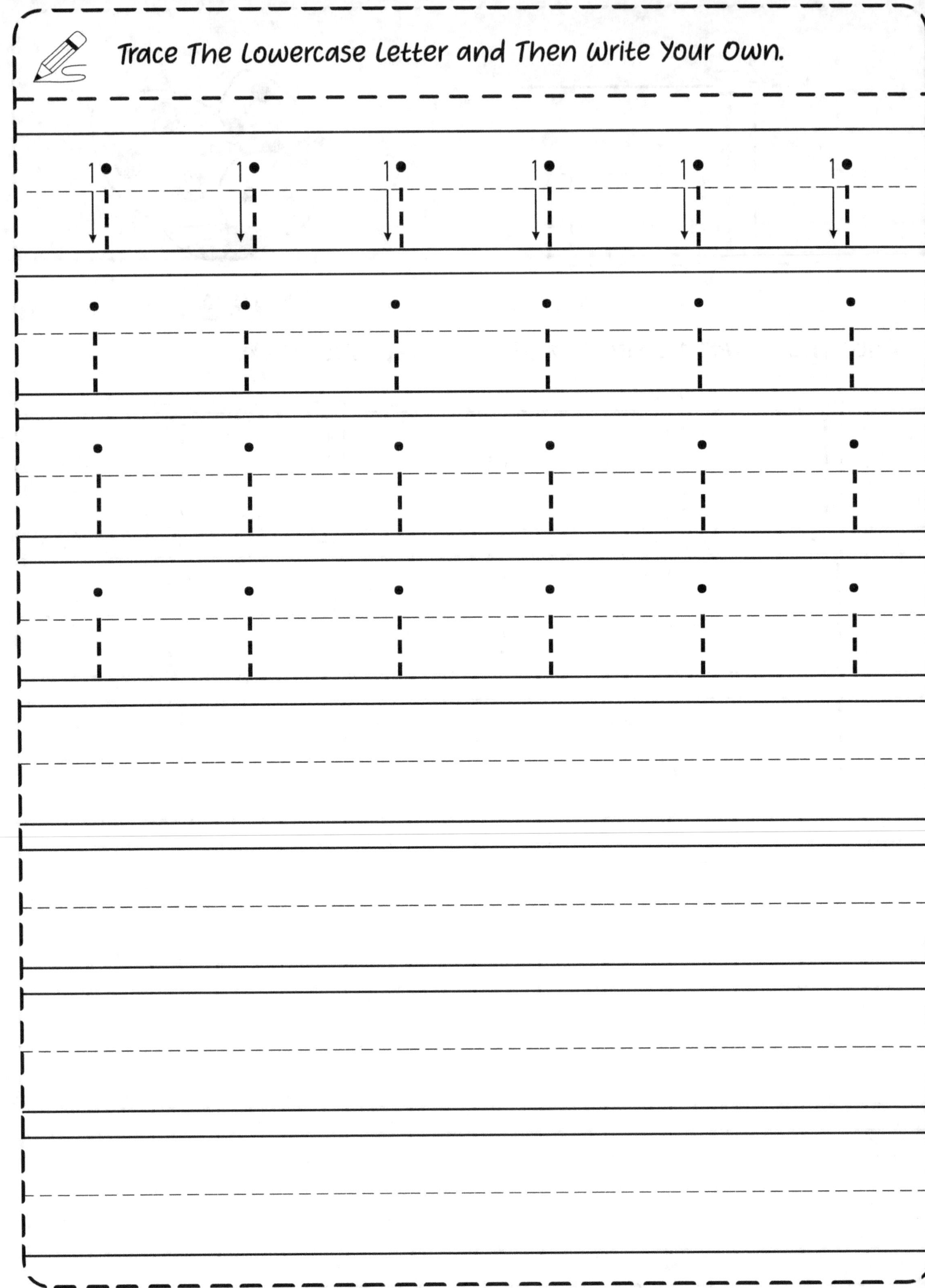

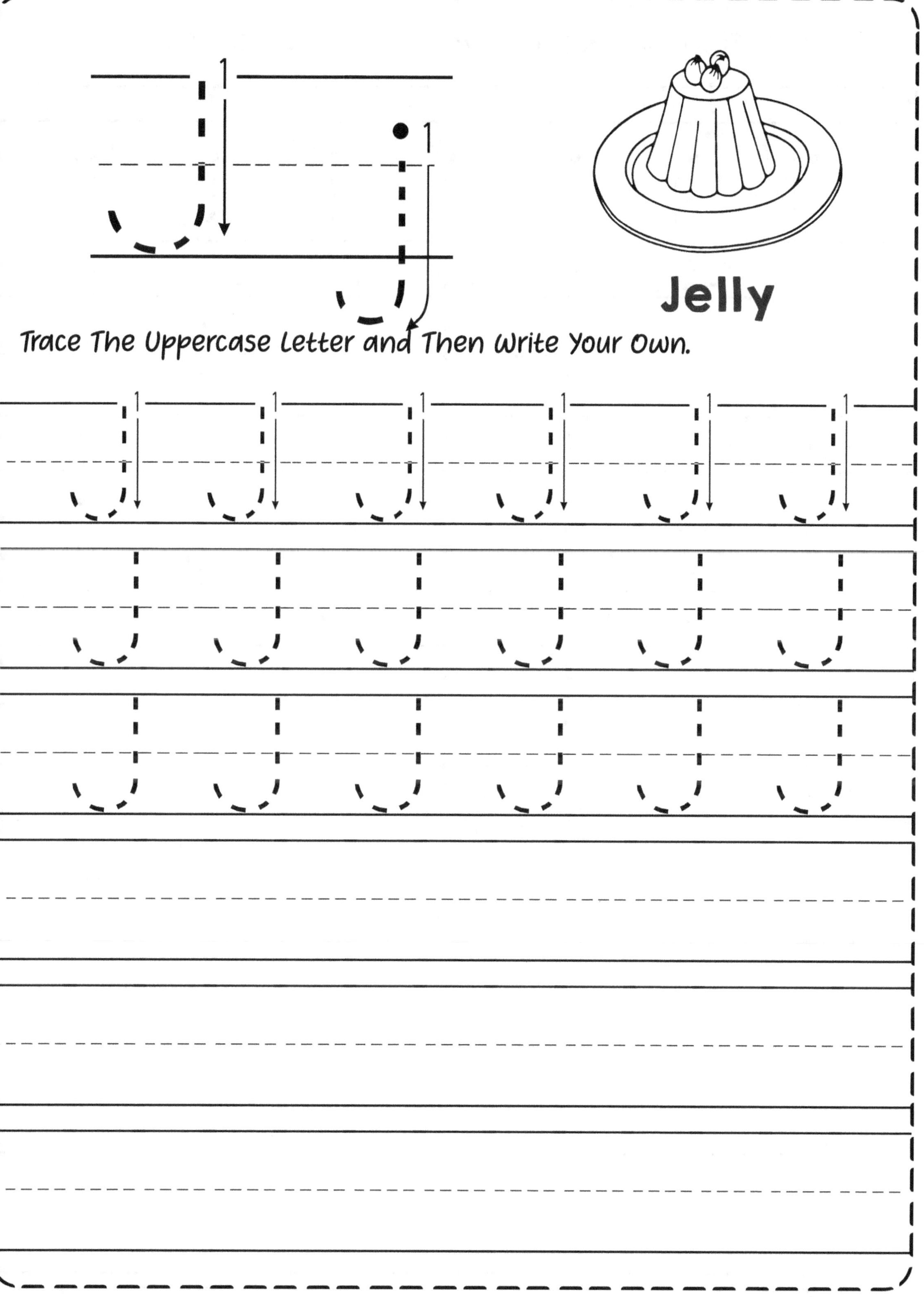

Trace The Uppercase Letter and Then Write Your Own.

Jelly

Trace The Lowercase Letter and Then Write Your Own.

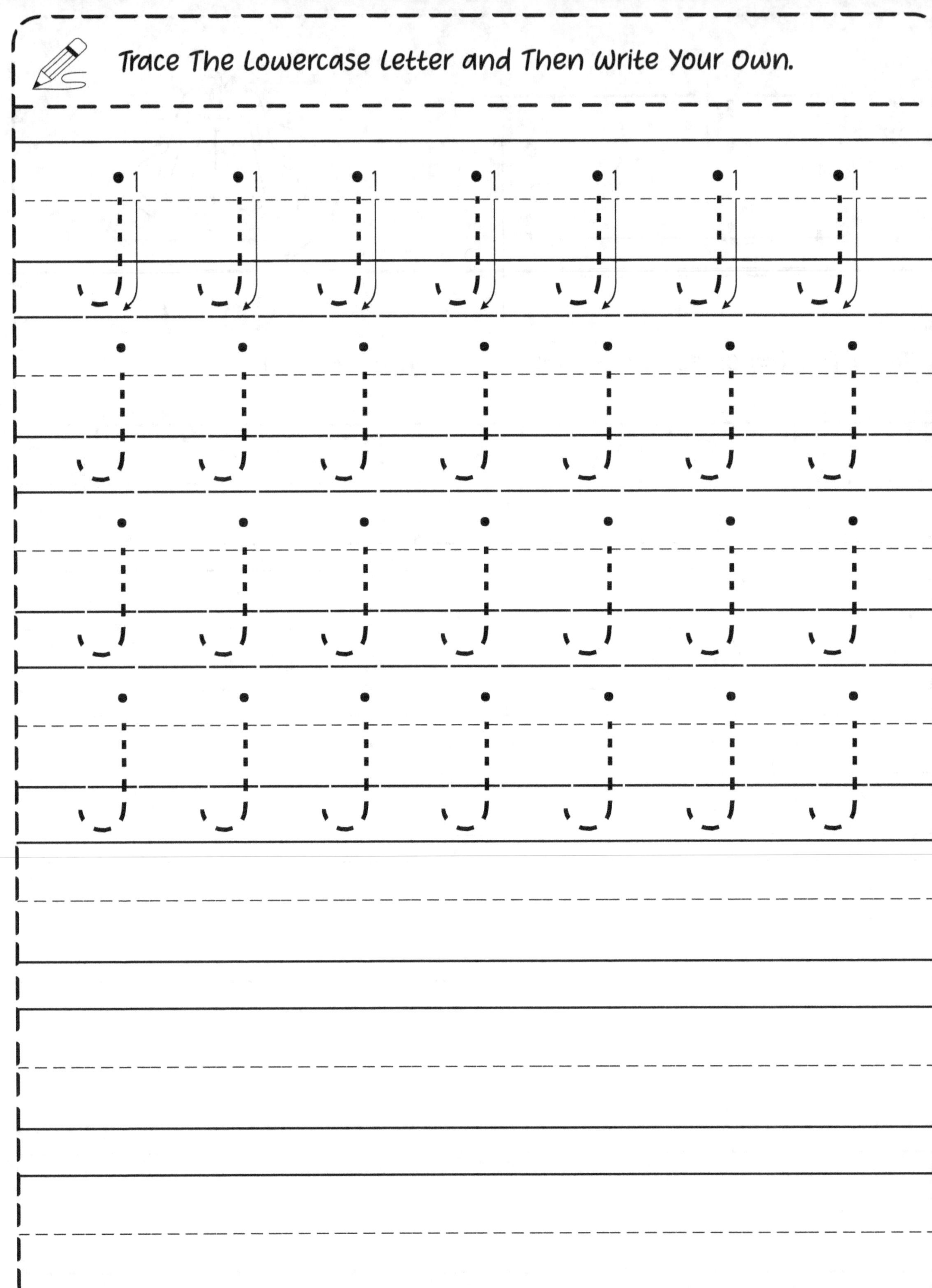

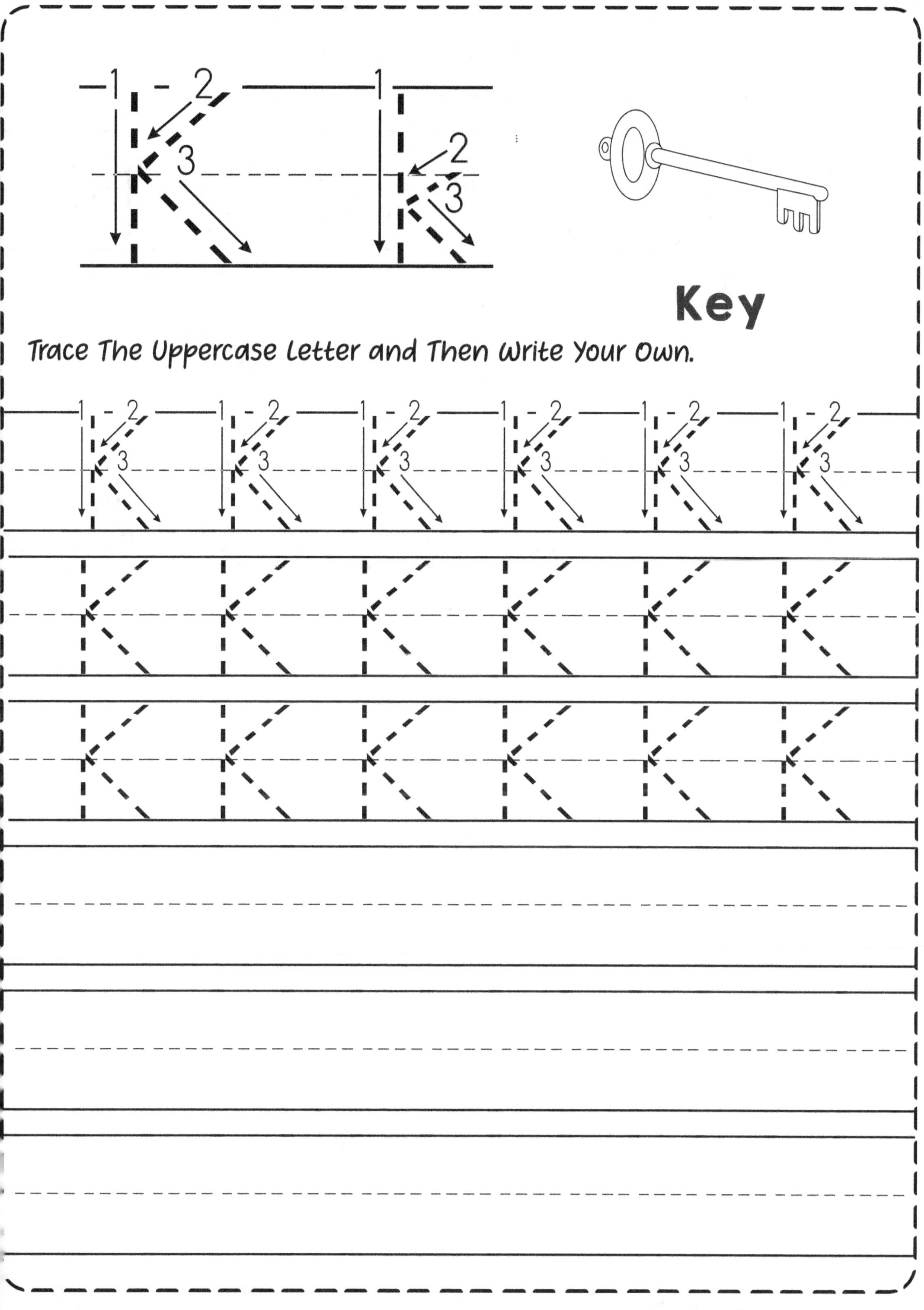

Key

Trace The Uppercase Letter and Then Write Your Own.

Trace The Lowercase Letter and Then Write Your Own.

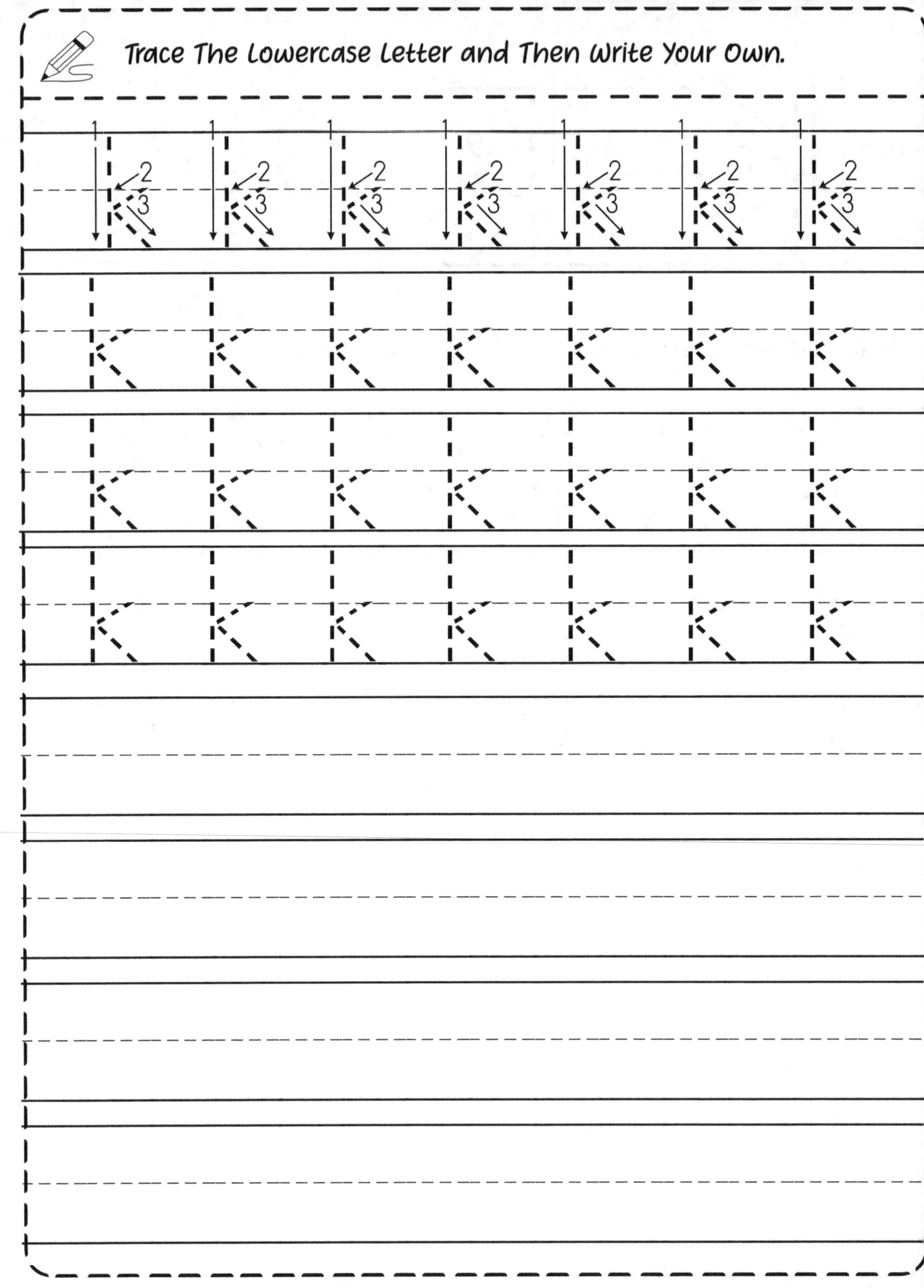

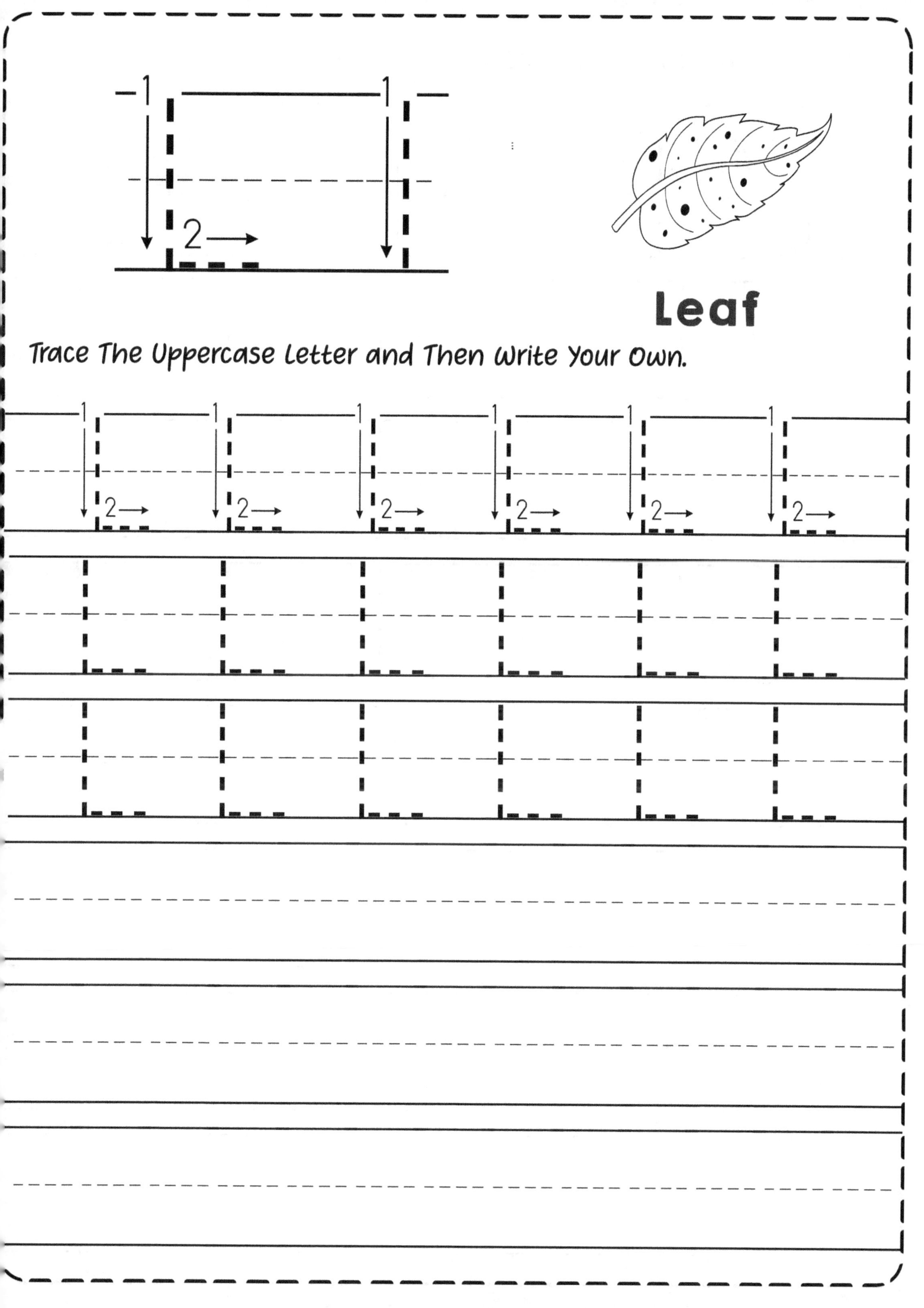

Leaf
Trace The Uppercase Letter and Then Write Your Own.

Trace The Lowercase Letter and Then Write Your Own.

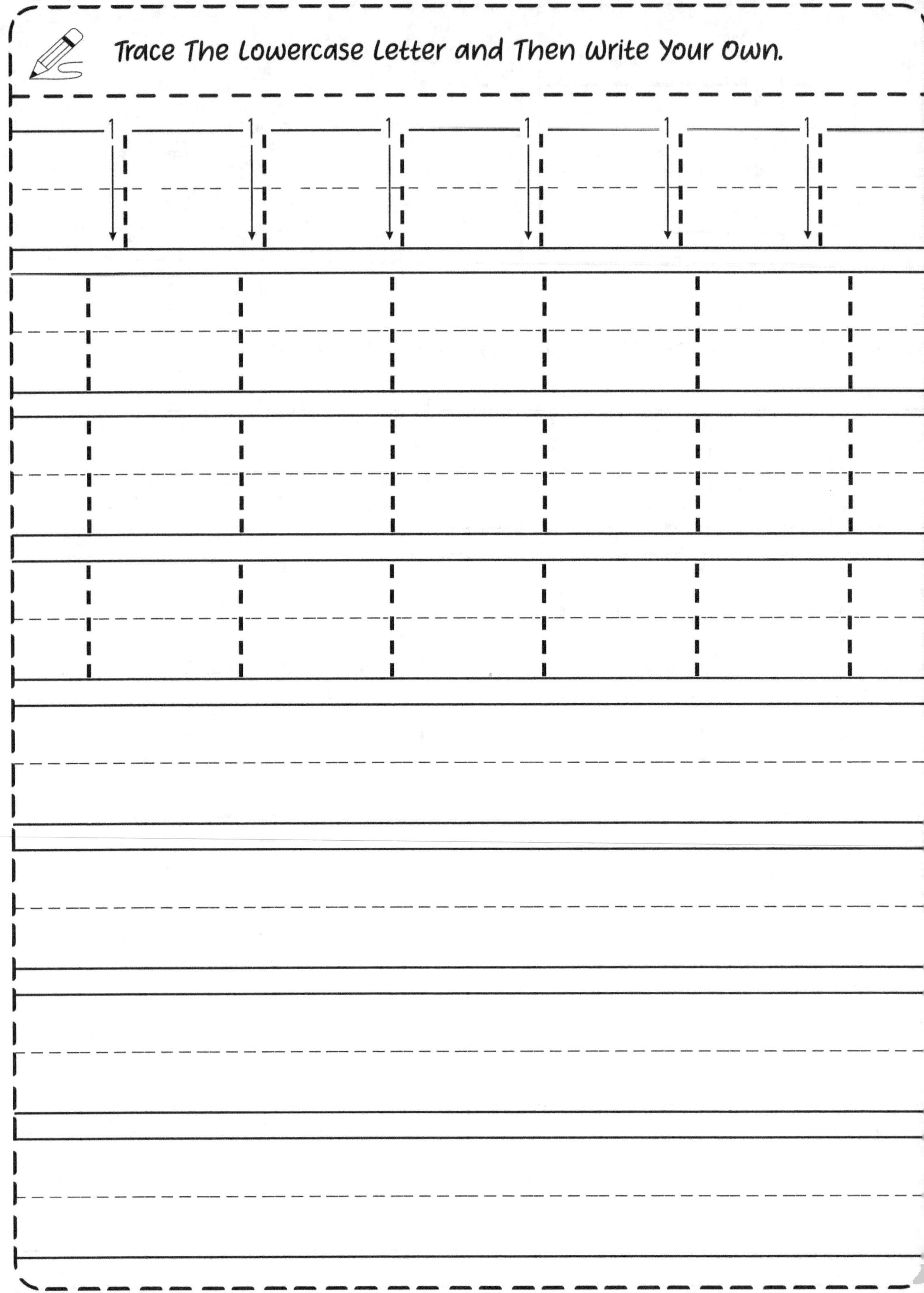

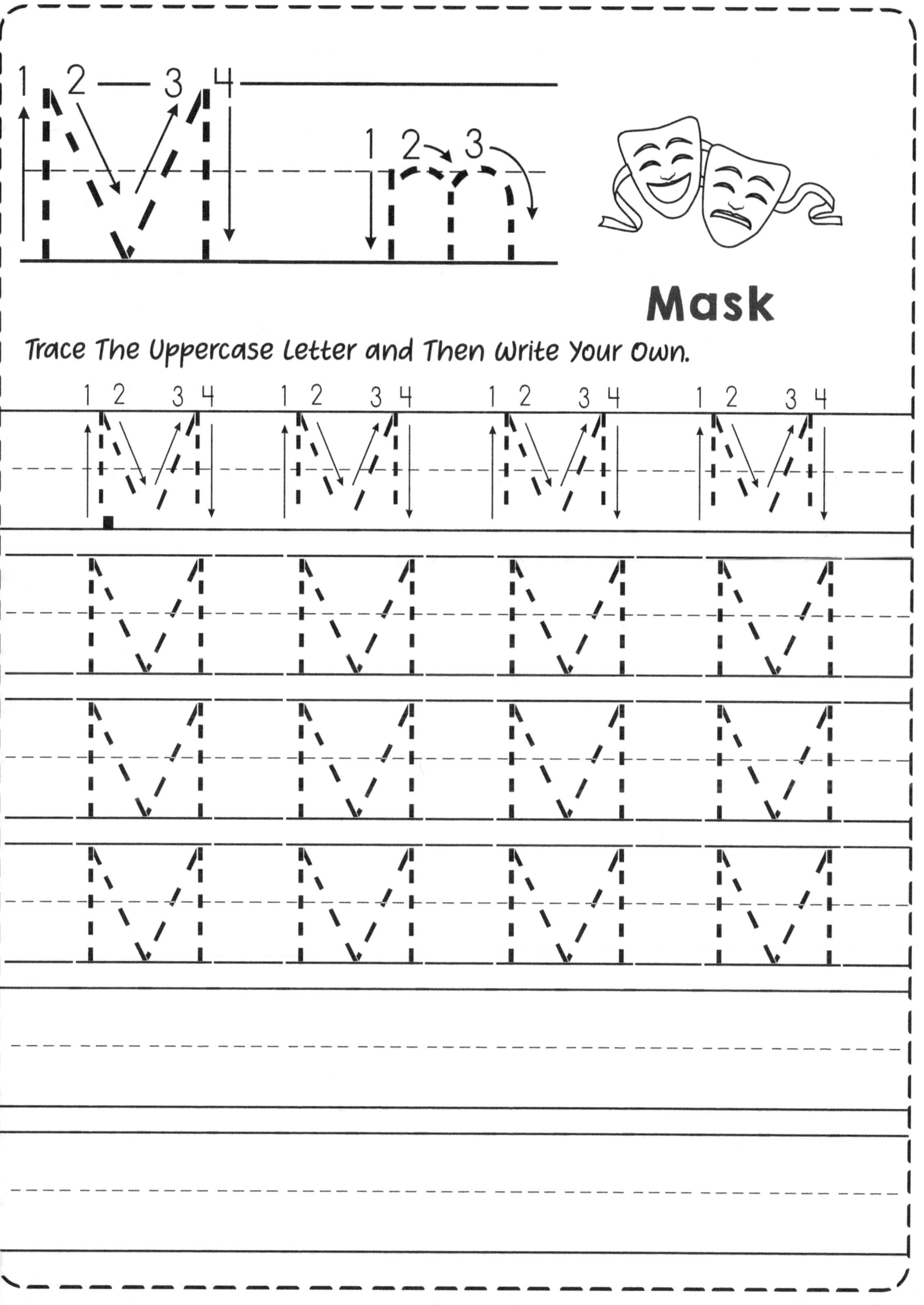

Mask

Trace The Uppercase Letter and Then Write Your Own.

Trace The Lowercase Letter and Then Write Your Own.
1 2 3   1 2 3   1 2 3   1 2 3   1 2 3

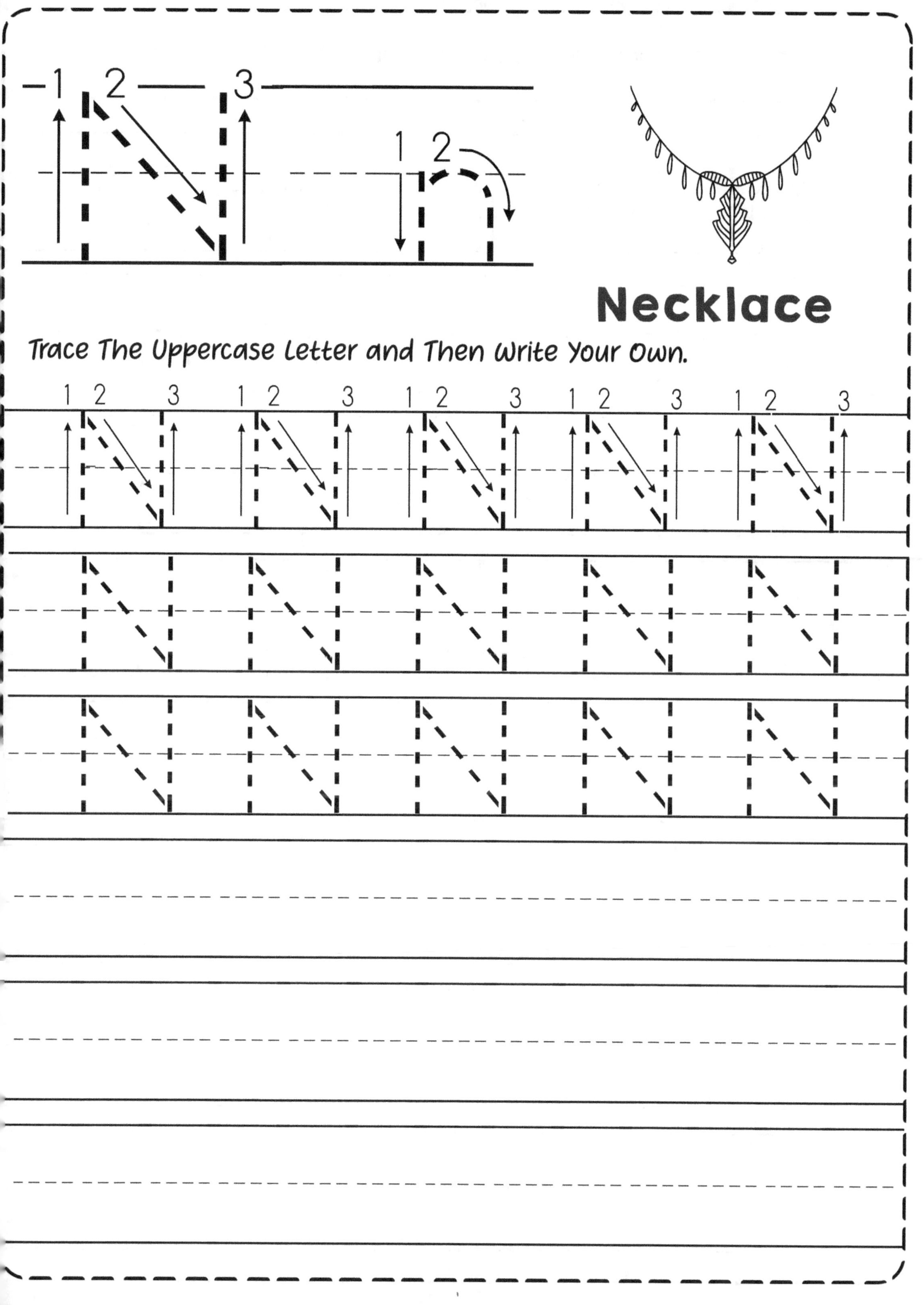
Necklace
Trace The Uppercase Letter and Then Write Your Own.

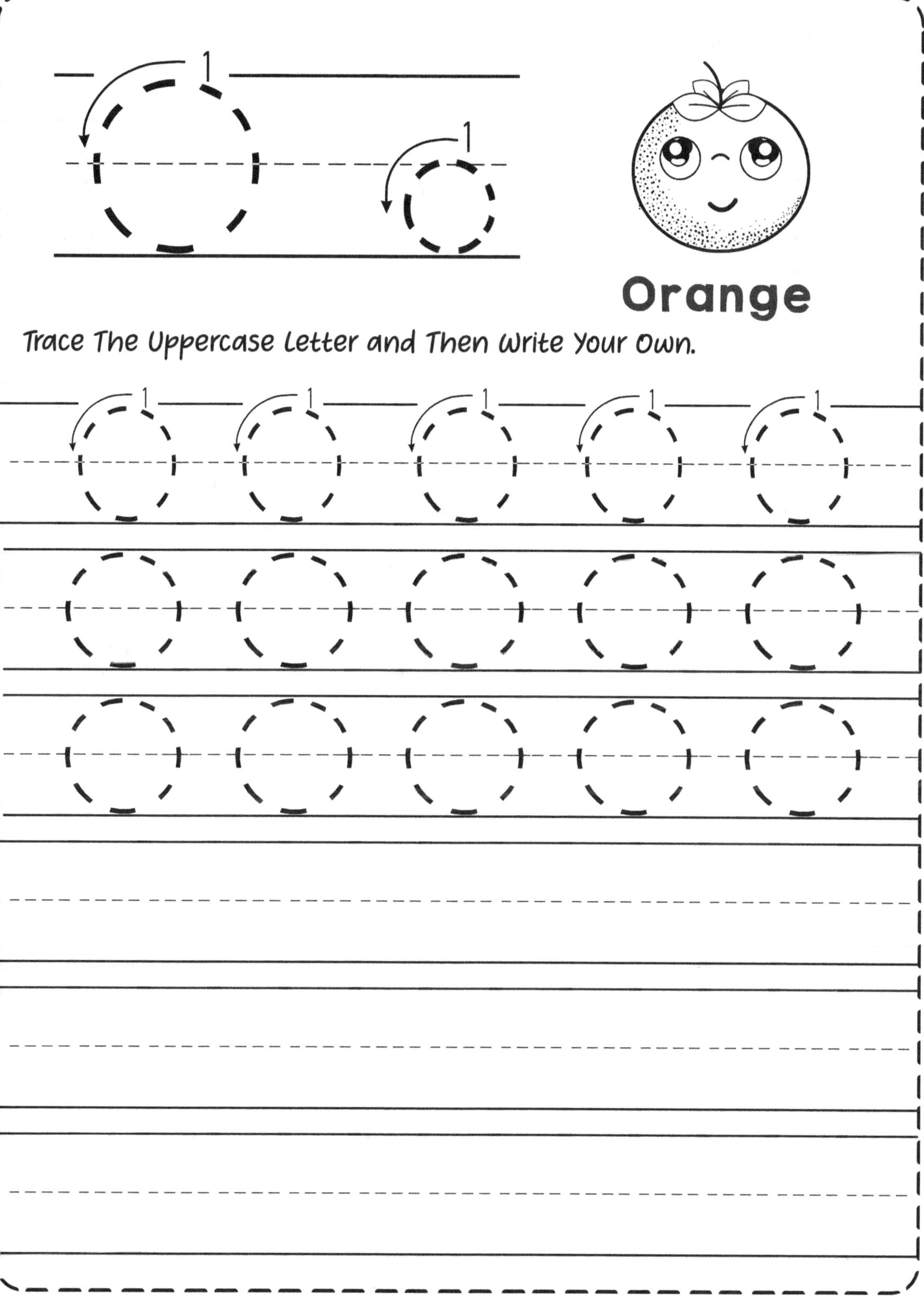

Orange
Trace The Uppercase Letter and Then Write Your Own.

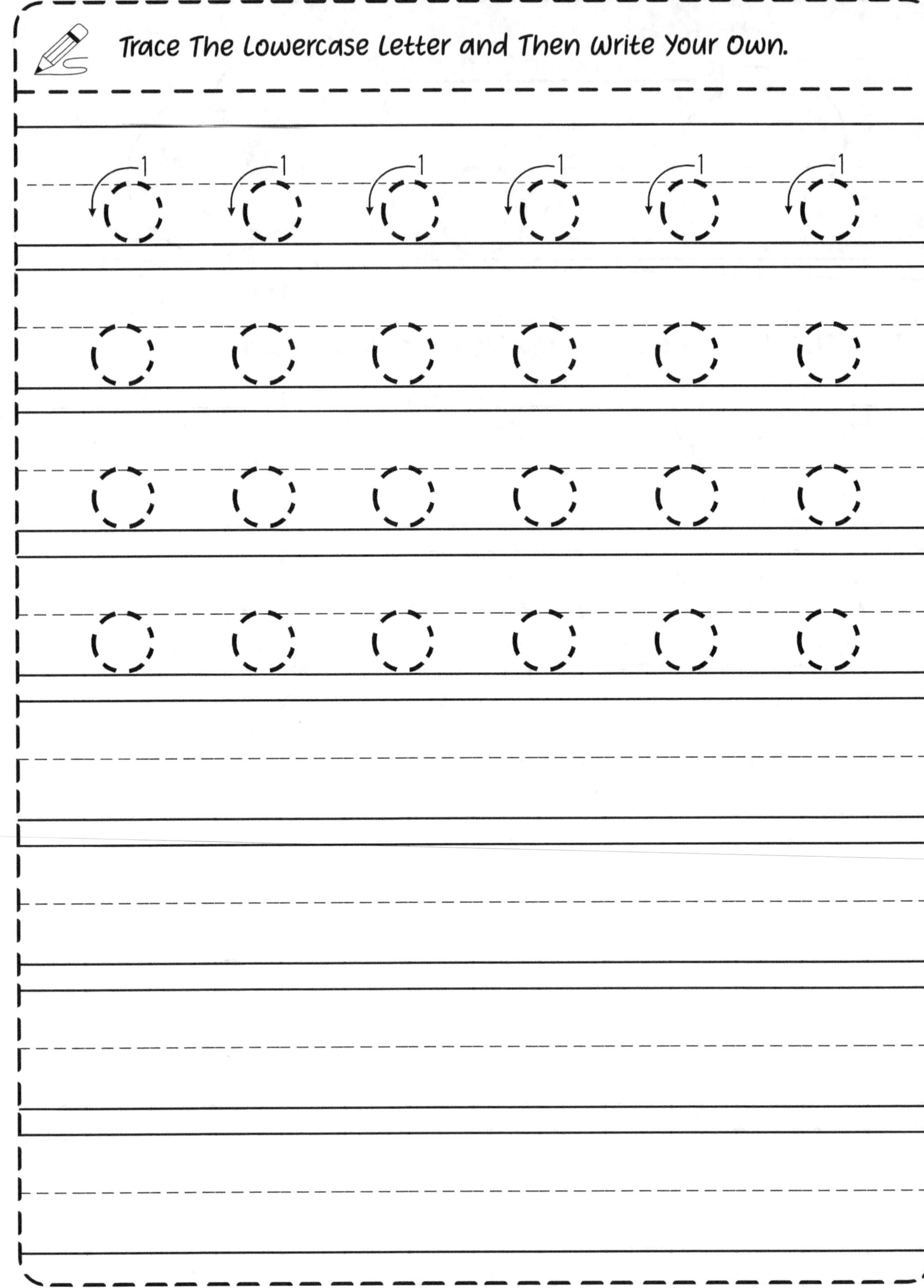
Trace The Lowercase Letter and Then Write Your Own.

Pear
Trace The Uppercase Letter and Then Write Your Own.

Trace The Lowercase Letter and Then Write Your Own.

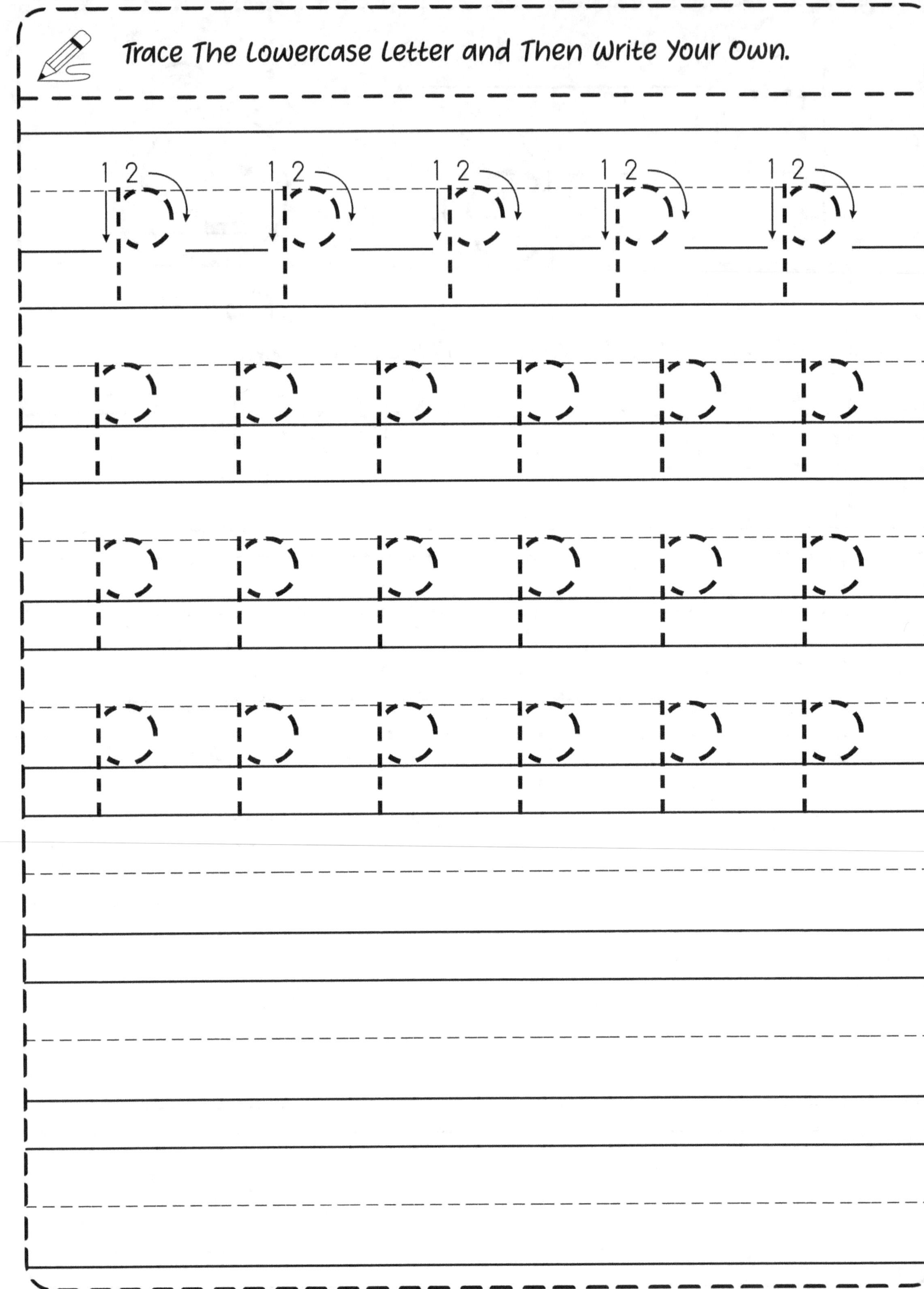

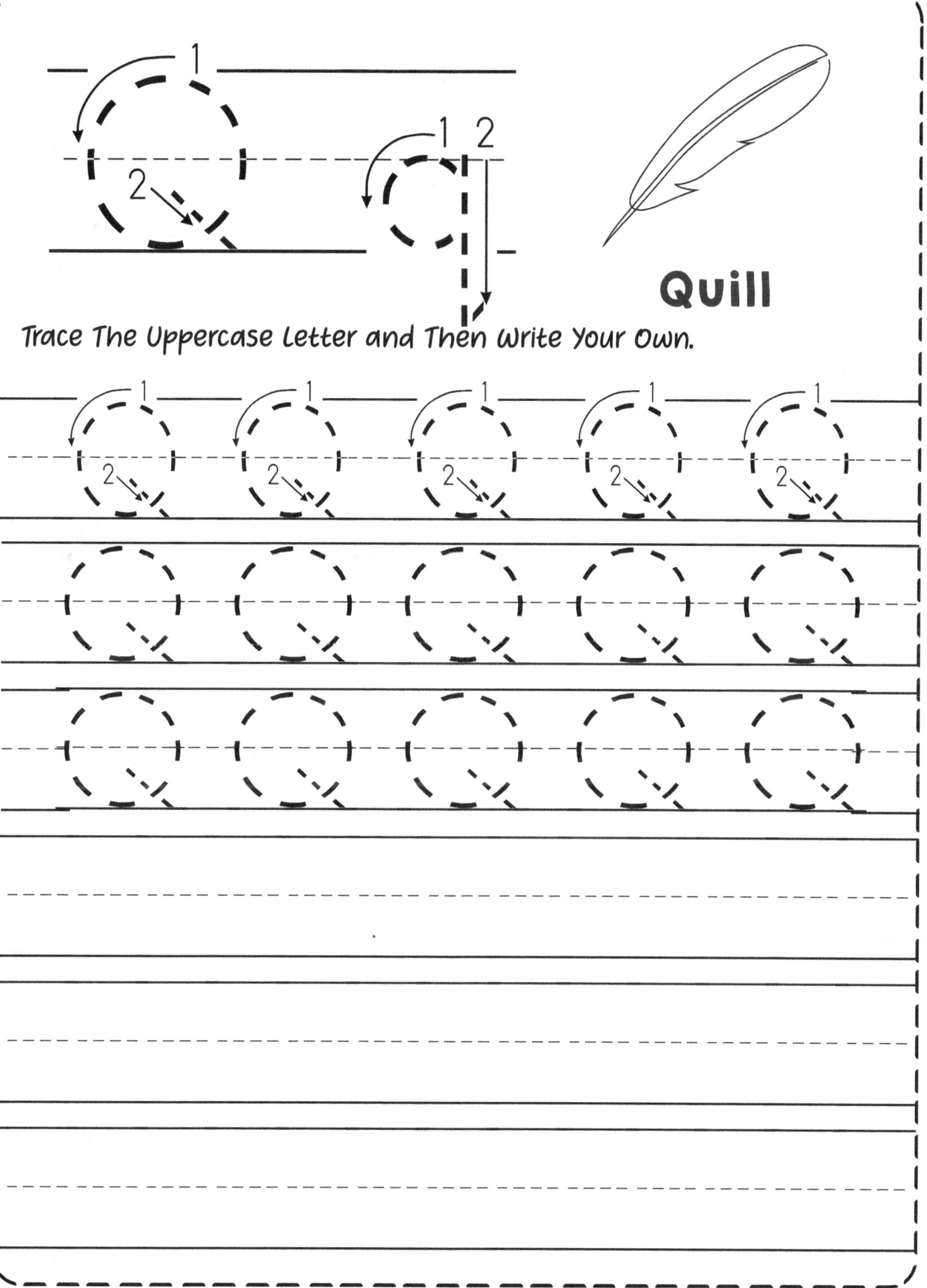

Quill
Trace The Uppercase Letter and Then Write Your Own.

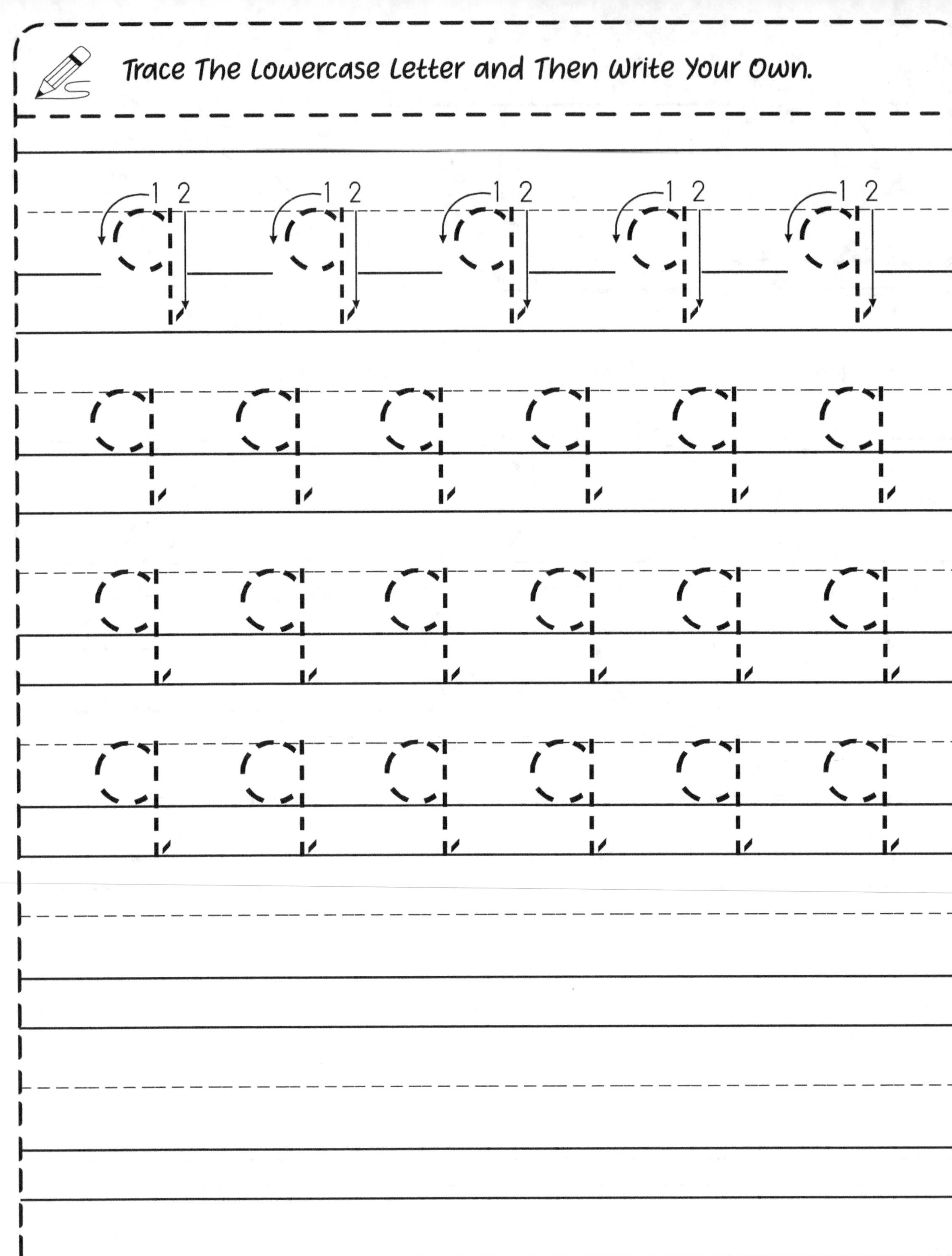

Trace The Lowercase Letter and Then Write Your Own.
1 2

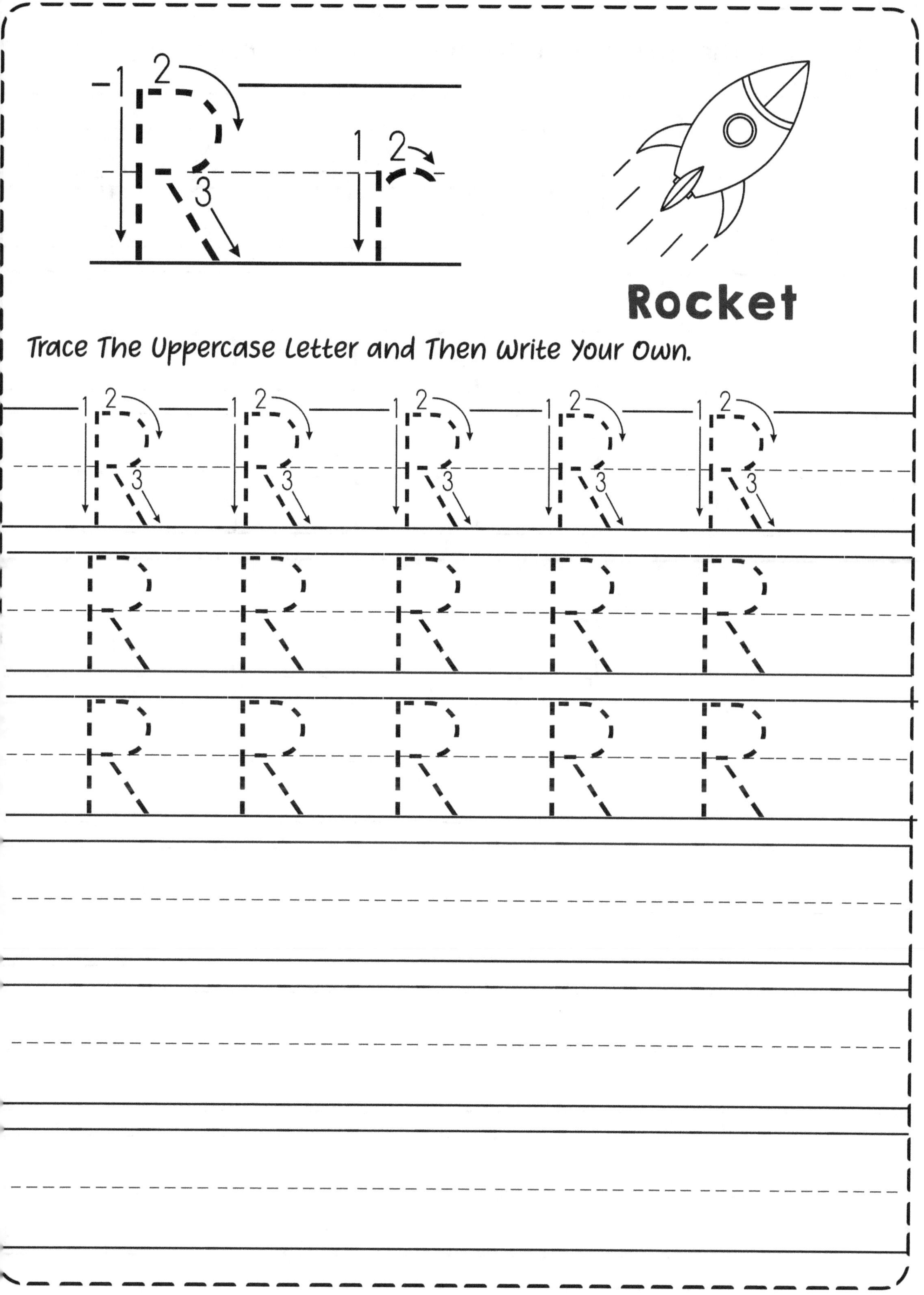

Rocket

Trace The Uppercase Letter and Then Write Your Own.

Trace The Lowercase Letter and Then Write Your Own.

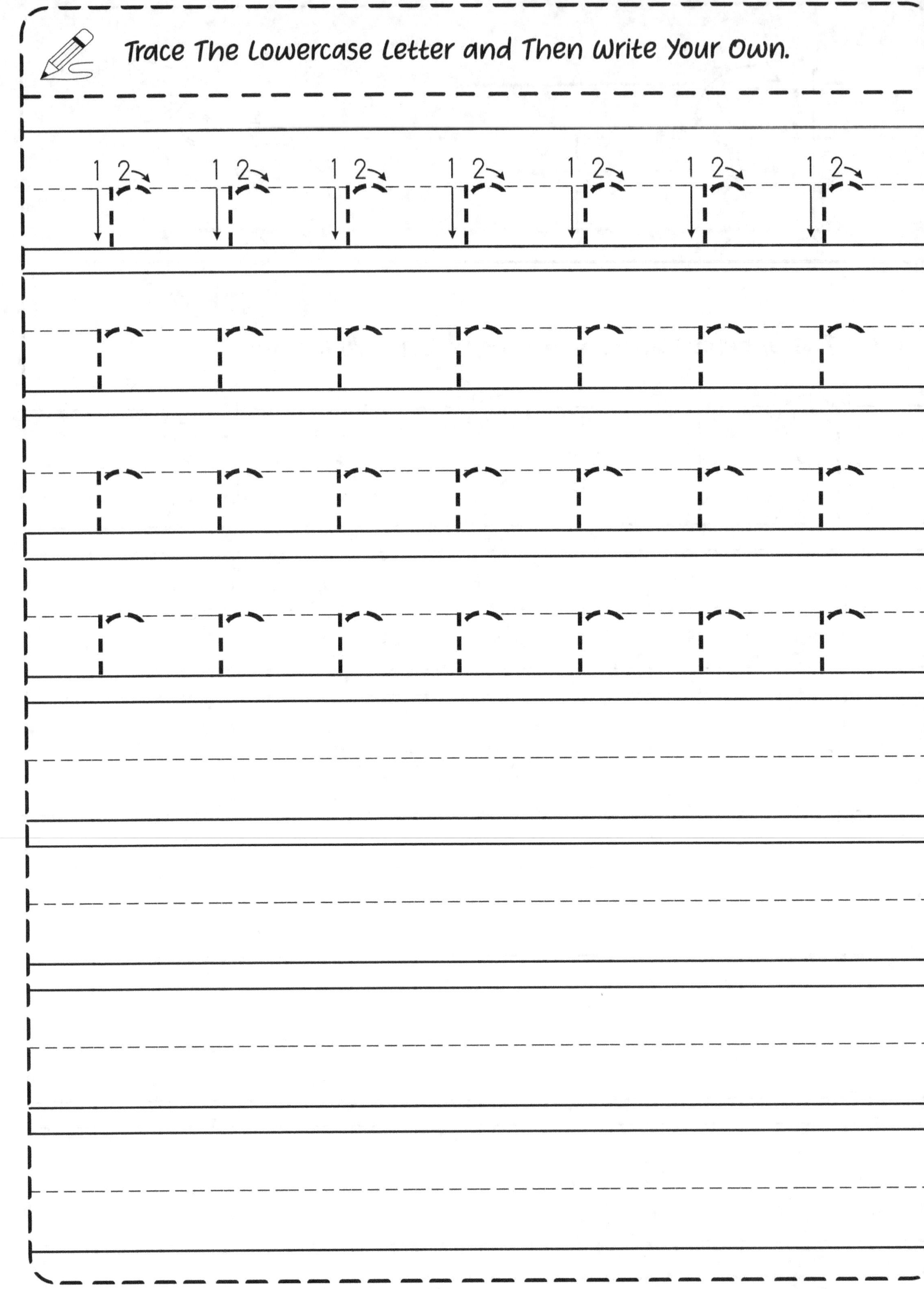

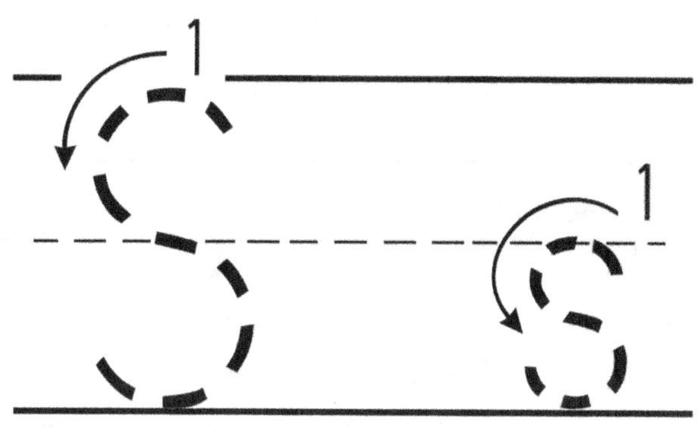

Strawberry

Trace The Uppercase Letter and Then Write Your Own.

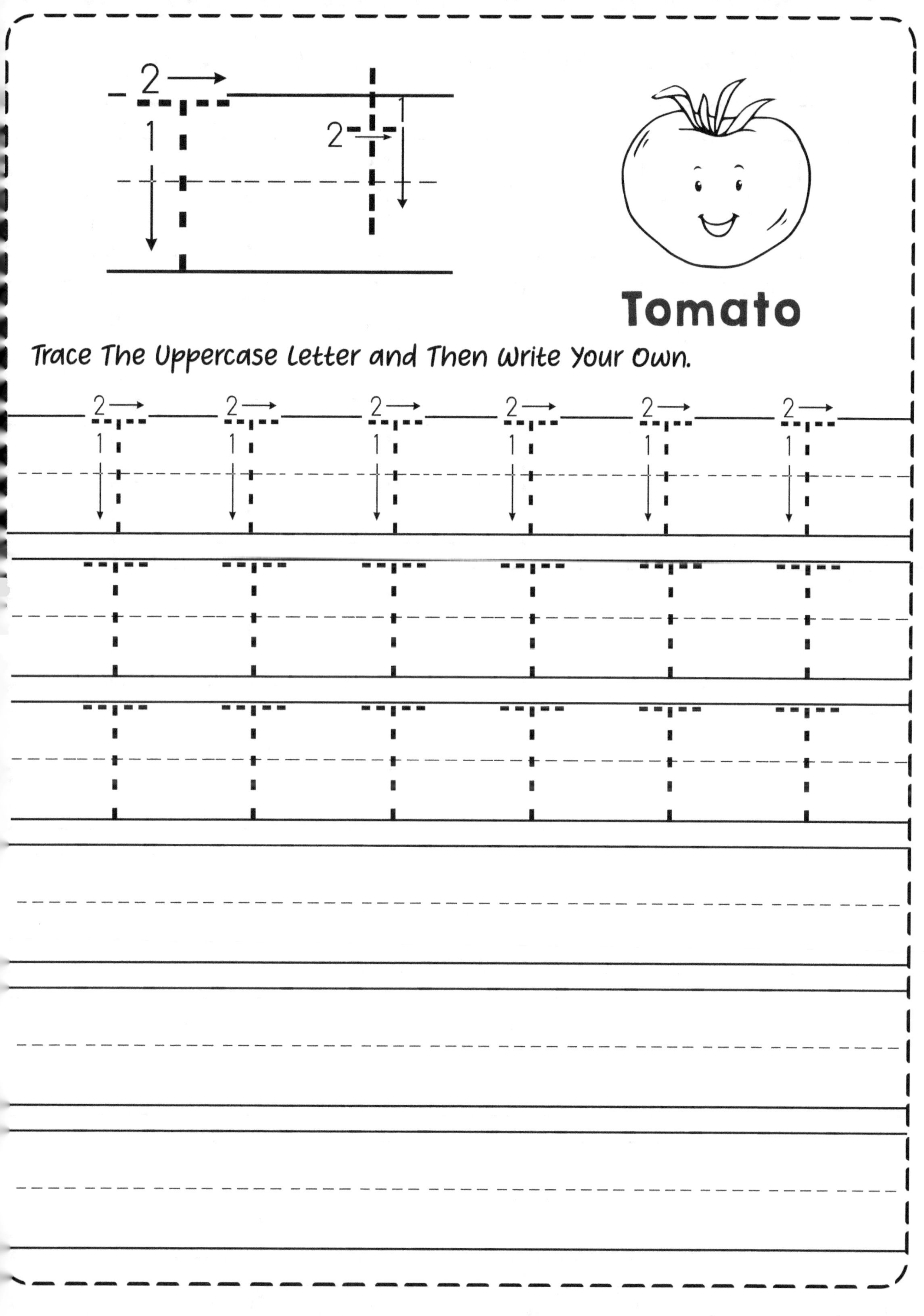

Tomato
Trace The Uppercase Letter and Then Write Your Own.

Trace The Lowercase Letter and Then Write Your Own.

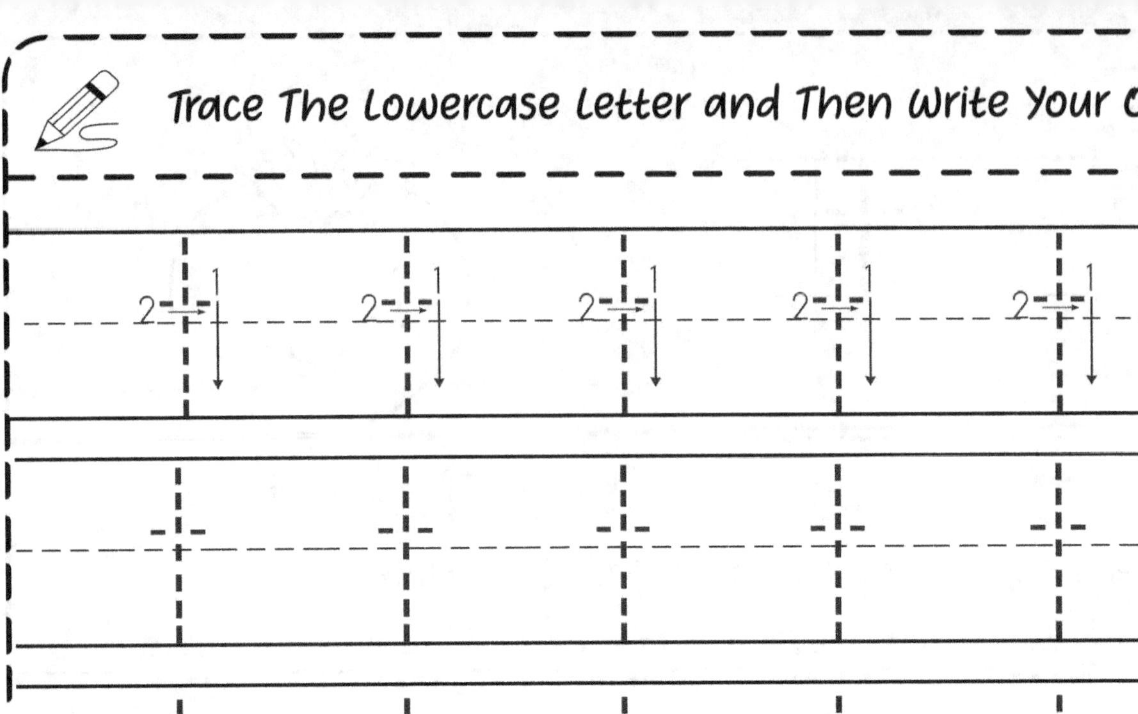

Unicorn

Trace The Uppercase Letter and Then Write Your Own.

Trace The Lowercase Letter and Then Write Your Own.

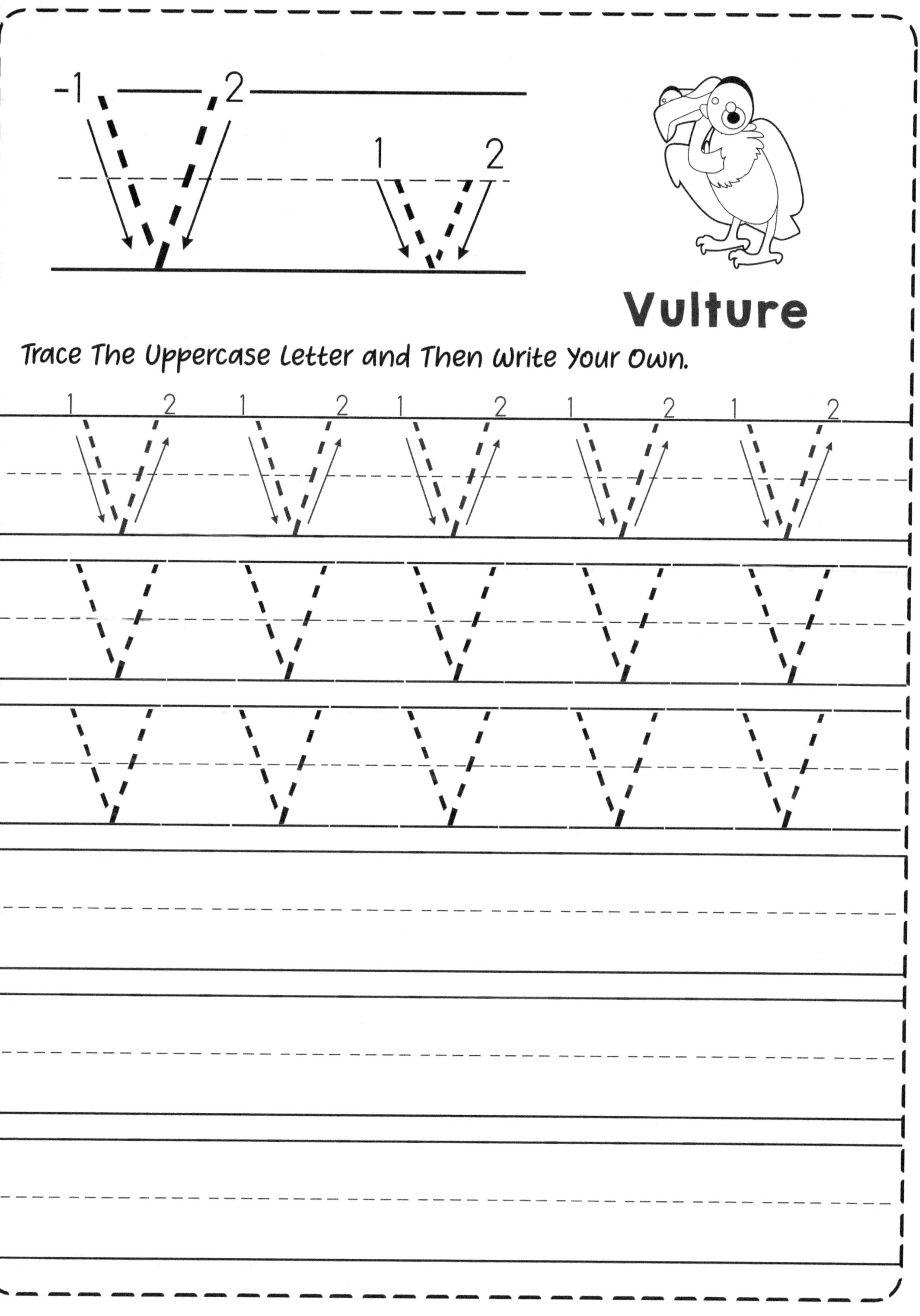

Vulture
Trace The Uppercase Letter and Then Write Your Own.

Trace The Lowercase Letter and Then Write Your Own.

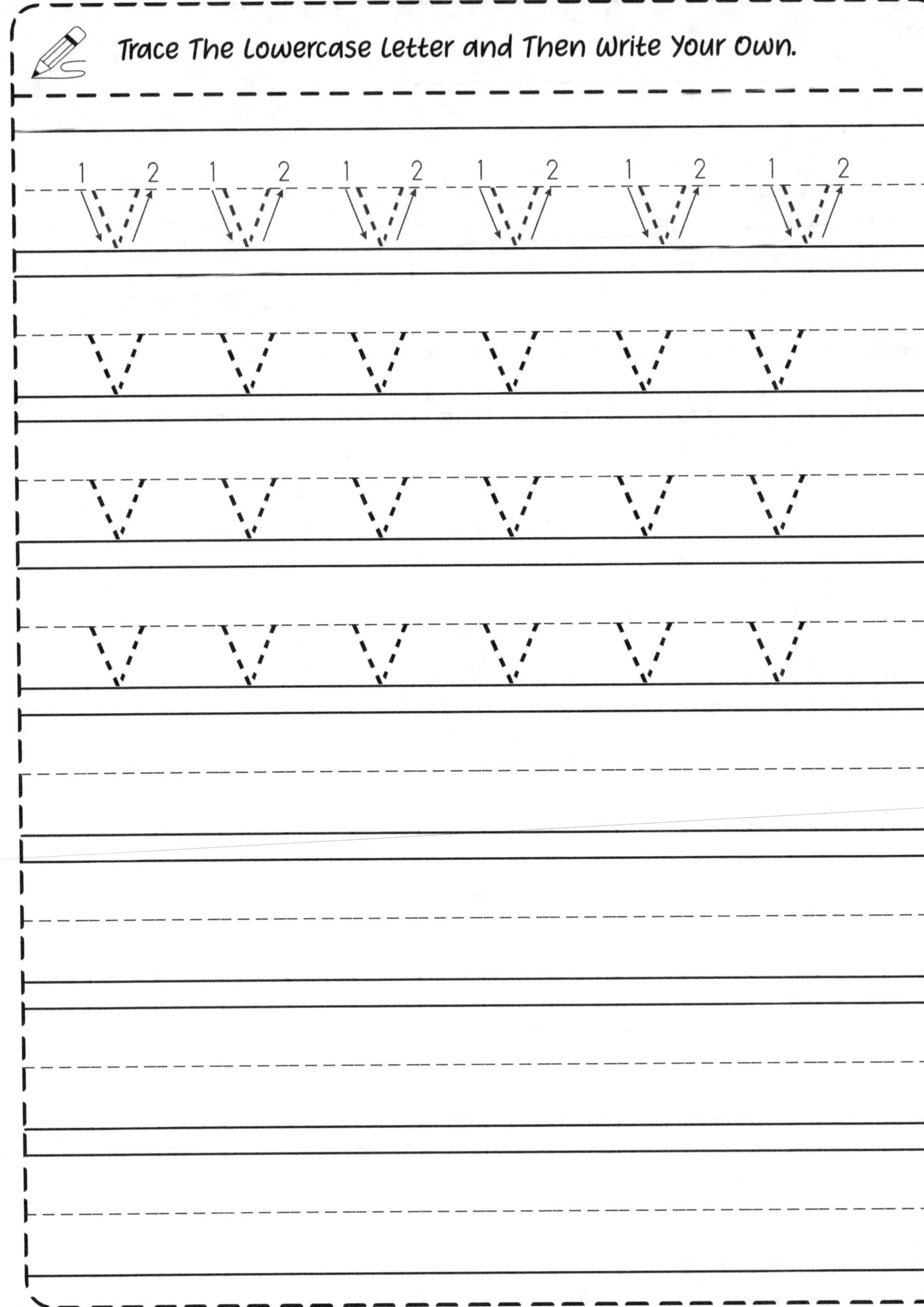

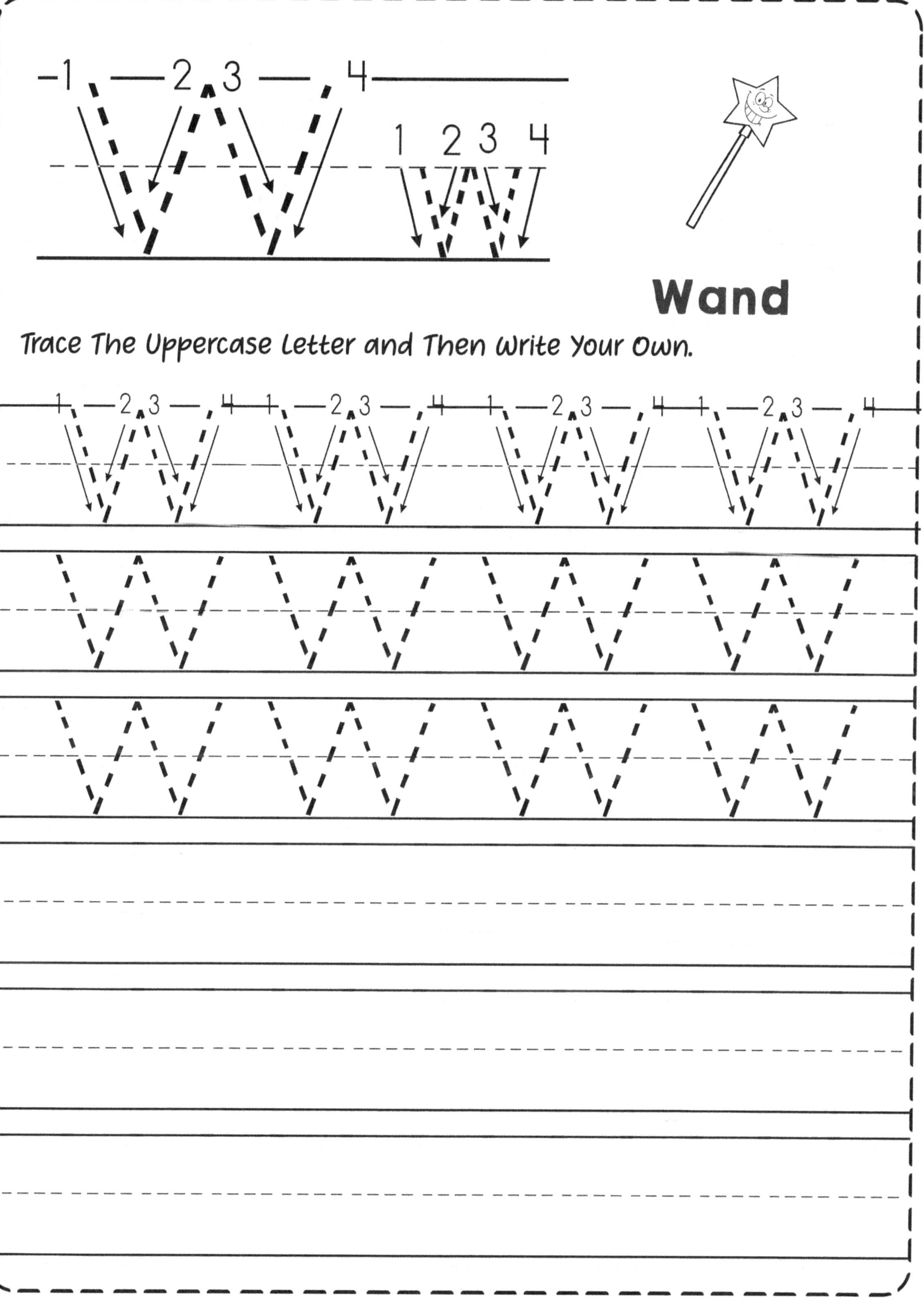

Wand

Trace The Uppercase Letter and Then Write Your Own.

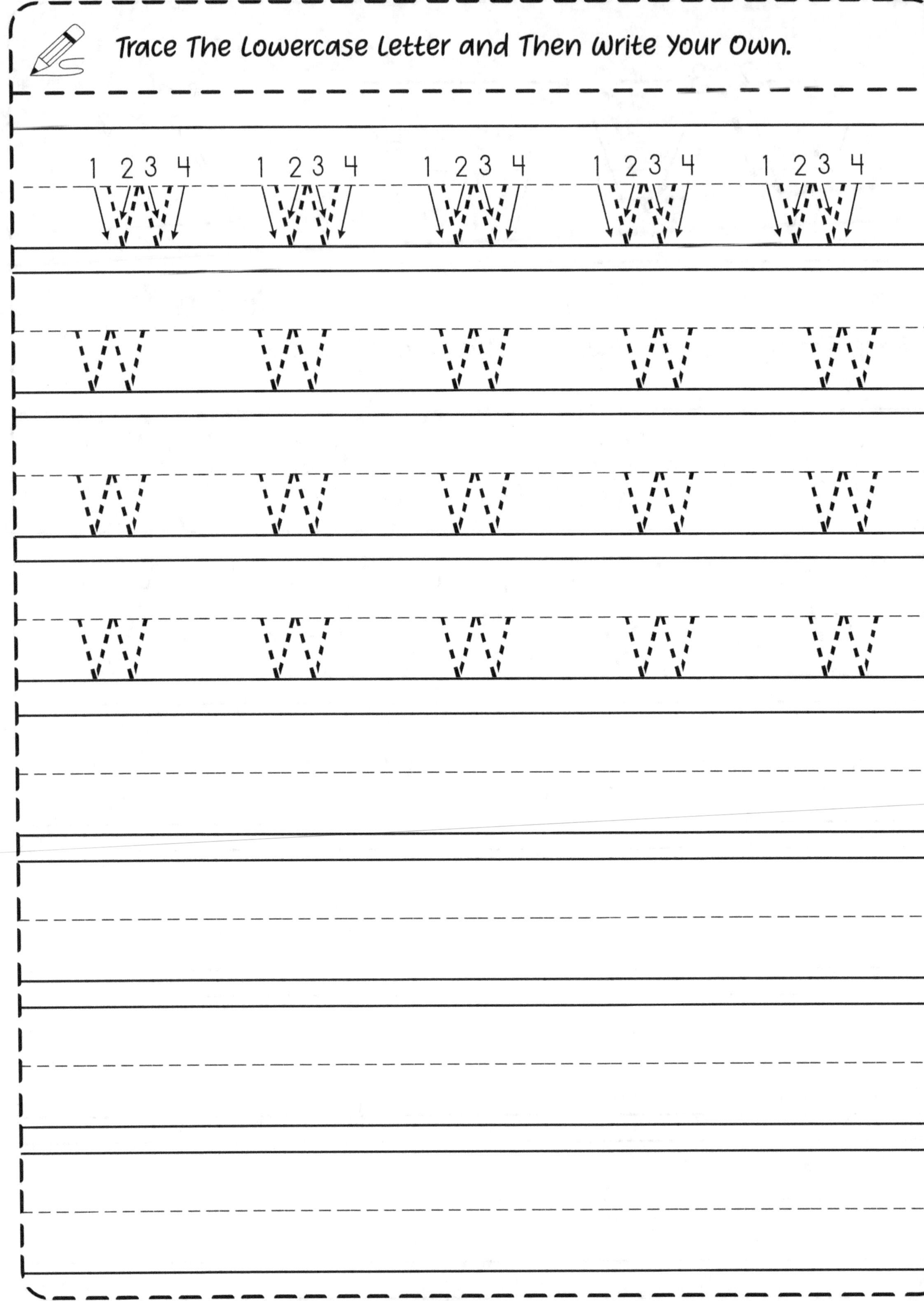Trace The Lowercase Letter and Then Write Your Own.
1 2 3 4   1 2 3 4   1 2 3 4   1 2 3 4   1 2 3 4

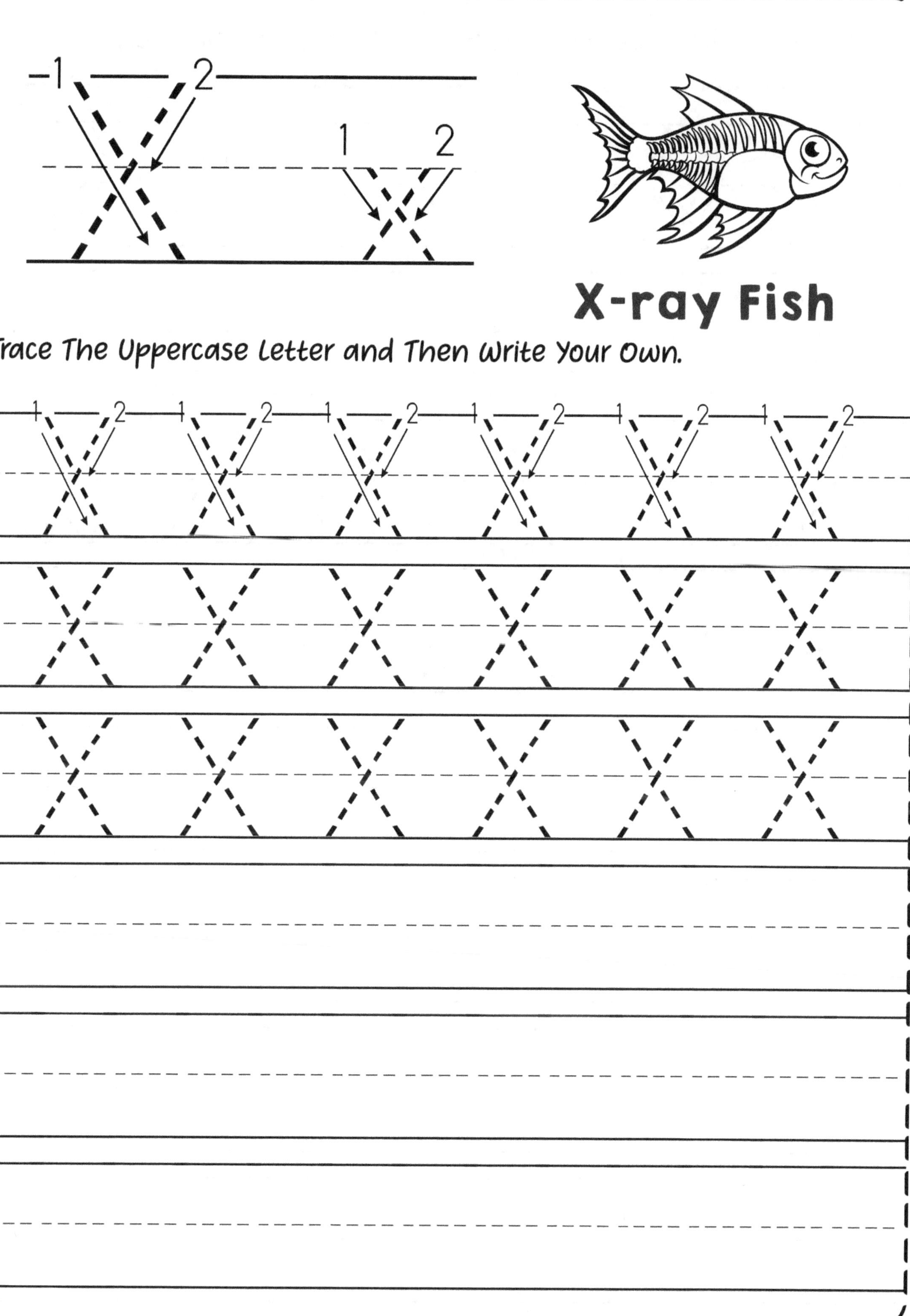

X-ray Fish
Trace The Uppercase Letter and Then Write Your Own.

Trace The Lowercase Letter and Then Write Your Own.
1 2 1 2 1 2 1 2 1 2 1 2 1 2

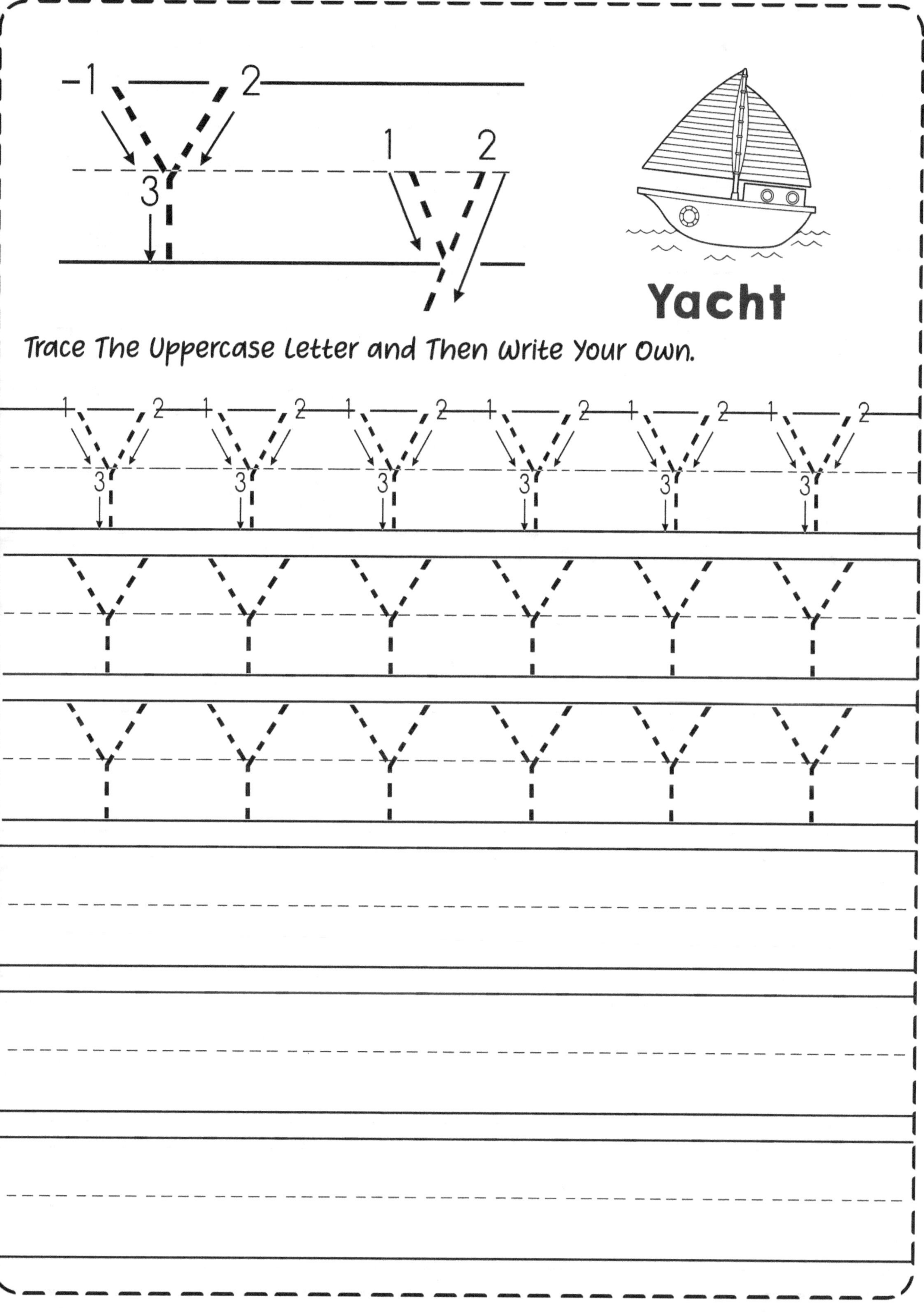

Yacht

Trace The Uppercase Letter and Then Write Your Own.

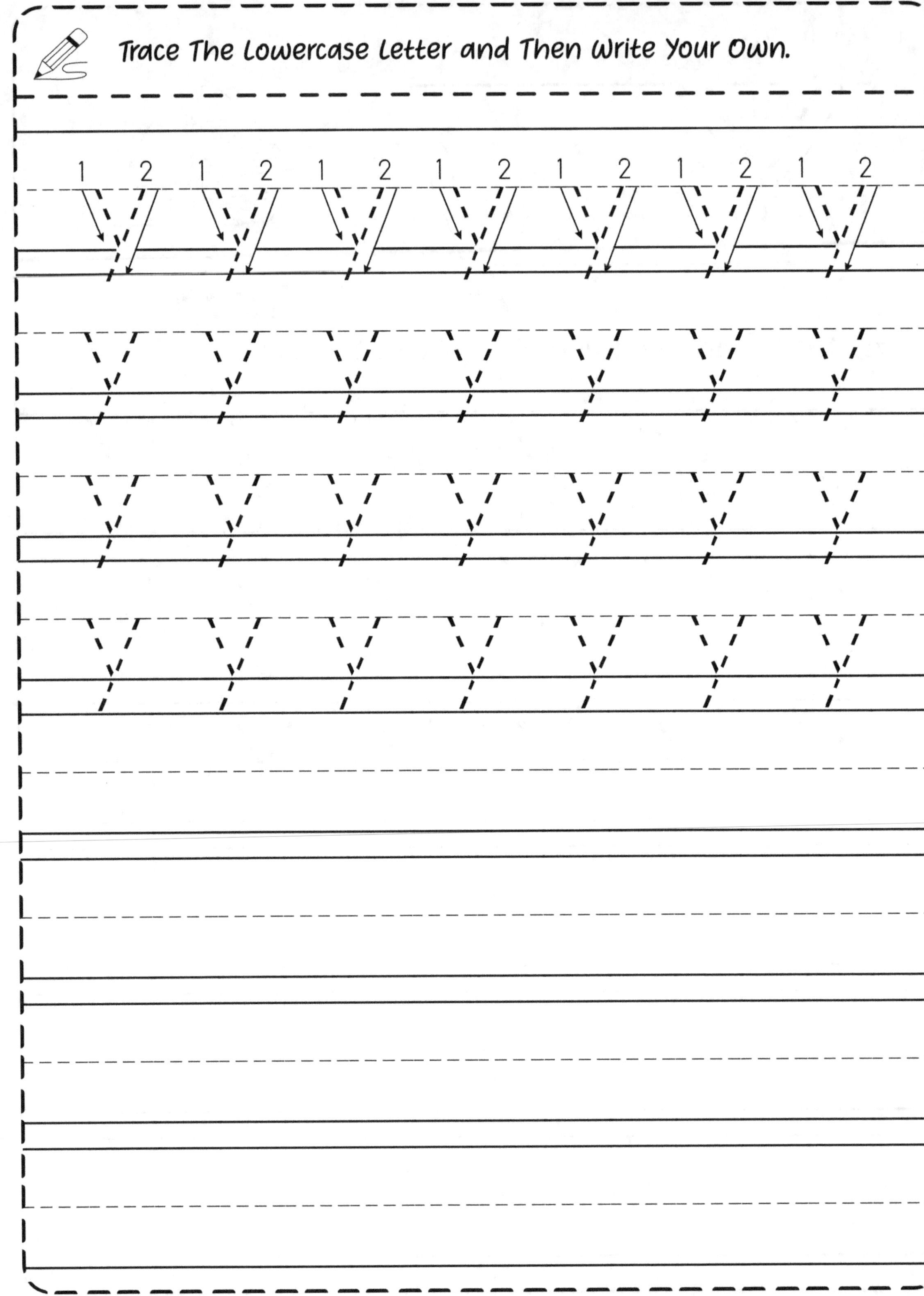

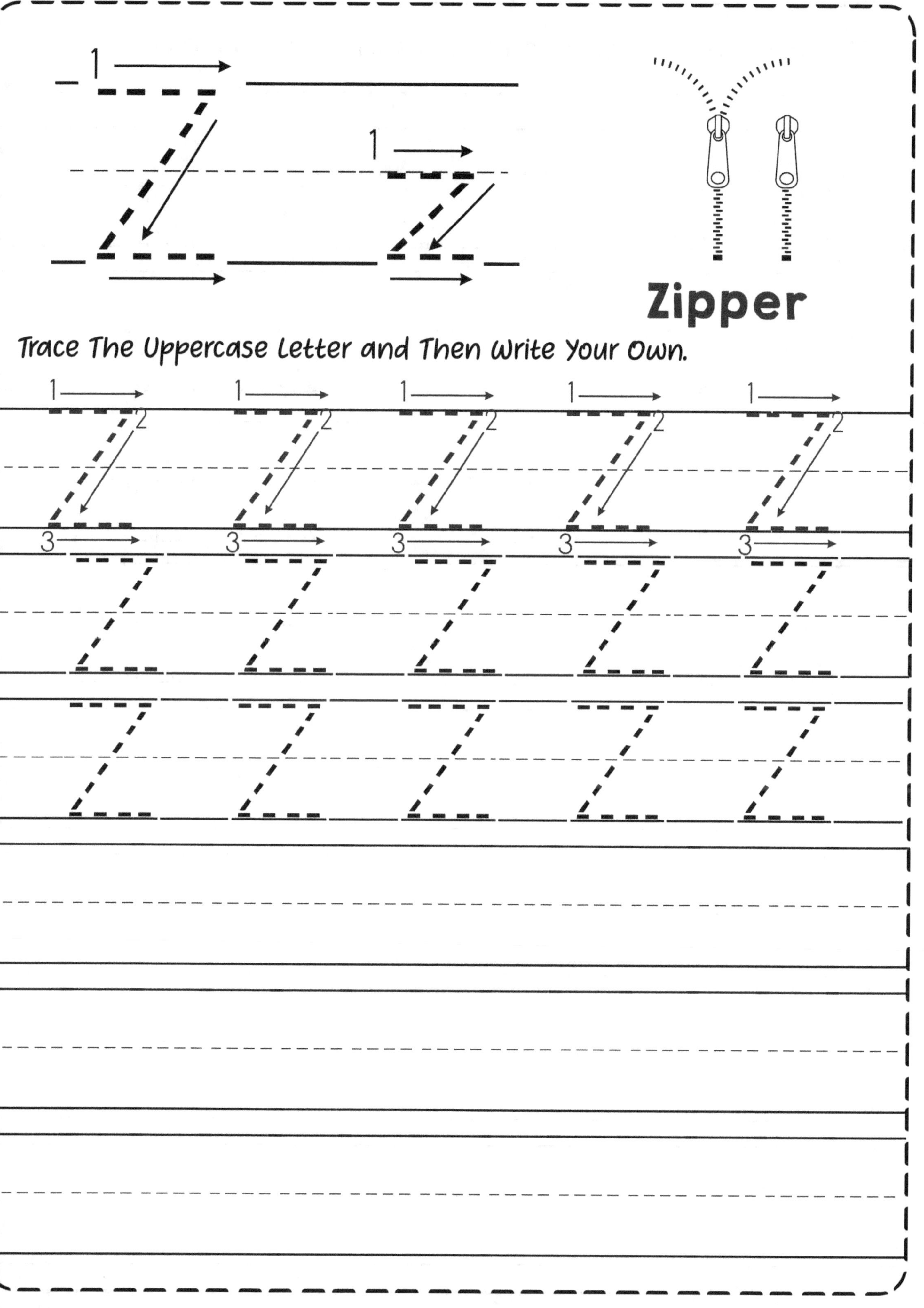

Trace The Uppercase Letter and Then Write Your Own.

Trace The Lowercase Letter and Then Write Your Own.